Angel Numbers
and
Divine Numerology

UNLOCKING THE MEANING
AND DIVINE MESSAGES OF
THE UNIVERSE

SARAH RIPLEY

Angel Numbers and Divine Numerology

Copyright © 2024 Sarah Ripley & Street Cat Publishing

All rights reserved.

No part of this book may be reproduced, distributed, or transmitted in any form or by any means, including photocopying, recording, or other electronic or mechanical methods, without the prior written permission of the publisher, except in the case of brief quotations embodied in critical reviews and certain other noncommercial uses permitted by copyright law.

Other Titles by
Sarah Ripley:

The 369 Project: A Manifestation Journal to Create the Life You Desire

The Shadow Work Journal: A Guide for Exploring your Hidden Self

101 Questions to ask Before you say "I Do"

The Lucky Girl Journal: A Guided Workbook for Manifesting your Dreams

Questions For Couples: 365 Questions to guide you to Stronger Communication, Trust and Intimacy

365 Daily AffirmationsFor Women: A Year fo Daily Affirmations to bring Peace, Joy and Happiness to your Life.

The Self-Love Workbook for Women: 90 Days to a More Loving and Accepting Relationship with Yourself

The Power of the 369 Method: Unlock the Cosmic Code and Create the Life you Desire using the Law of Attraction

Dive deeper into the world of Angel Numbers with exclusive bonus content.

Scan the QR code to receive your 5 FREE Angel Numbers Journal Pages!

Table of Contents

Introduction 6
Angel Number 0 14
Angel Number 1 18
Angel Number 2 22
Angel Number 3 26
Angel Number 4 30
Angel Number 5 34
Angel Number 6 38
Angel Number 7 42
Angel Number 8 46
Angel Number 9 50
Angel Numbers 0-999 54

Introduction

Imagine a world swirling with uncertainty, where every turn feels like a blind step. It's in these moments that many seek a guiding hand, a whisper of reassurance from the universe. And that's where angel numbers step in – those mysterious repeating sequences that seem to wink at you from clocks, receipts, and license plates.

These aren't just numbers, they're echoes from the universe, gentle nudges from angels or the cosmos itself. They're like little lighthouses in the storm, reminding you that you're not lost in the dark, that there's a bigger plan unfolding even when you can't see it. They're a secret code, just for you, whispering words of encouragement, like "You're on the right track," or "Keep going, you've got this."

Why do these celestial messages resonate so deeply? Maybe it's like finding a four-leaf clover – a tiny spark of magic in the ordinary. Maybe it's like receiving a handwritten letter from a loved one – a reminder that you're cared for, even in the distance. Whatever it is, angel numbers touch our hearts and stir our souls, reminding us that we're not alone in this grand adventure called life.

So, how do we decipher these cosmic whispers? Some people turn to numerology, an ancient art that sees numbers as humming with their own unique energy. When these numbers dance together in repeating sequences, they tell a story, a personal message that guides you towards growth and discovery. Others find meaning in the personal connections they forge with these numbers, like a lucky lottery ticket or a special birthday date. It's like these sequences become secret codes, whispers just for them, making the message even more powerful.

But remember, these angel numbers aren't magic spells or fortune cookies. They're gentle nudges to remind you of your inner strength, to spark your intuition, and to whisper words of encouragement.

Ultimately, the beauty of angel numbers lies in their ability to ignite our wonder and connect us to something bigger than ourselves. They're a reminder that even in the chaos, there's a magical thread woven into the fabric of existence. So, the next time you see a repeating number, take a moment. Listen. Let it guide you on your own unique and wondrous path.

What are Angel numbers?

Ever feel like the universe is sending you secret messages? Like there's a hidden code woven into the everyday – on clock faces, car tags, maybe even your morning latte receipt? Those sneaky little sequences, those repeating numbers whispering in the corner of your vision? Well, my friend, you might be tapping into the world of angel numbers!

Think of them as celestial winks, divine nudges from your angels or spirit guides. They're a way for these unseen guardians to reach out, offering a word of encouragement, a gentle nudge in the right direction, or maybe even a cosmic pat on the back. These numbers can pop up anywhere – a clock stuck on 11:11, a dream filled with 444s, or maybe that license plate flashing 777 as you pass by.

So, why are you suddenly seeing these numerical oddities? It could be a sign that your angels are trying to get your attention, whispering wisdom just for you. Maybe you're facing a big decision and they're sending you a little "trust your gut" nudge. Or perhaps you're feeling lost and they're reminding you that you're on the right path, even if it doesn't always feel like it.

The key is to pay attention. When you see those repeating numbers, take a moment to tune into your thoughts and feelings. What were you thinking about just then? What's going on in your life right now? These clues can help you unlock the secret message your angels are sending. Think of it like cracking a celestial code!

So, next time you see a suspicious string of numbers, don't just brush it off. It could be your angels or spirit guides sending you a special message, a little celestial love letter just for you. And who knows, maybe with a little open-mindedness and some heart-listening, you can crack the code and discover the secret guidance hiding in plain sight. Remember, the universe whispers, but sometimes, those whispers come disguised as numbers. Just have to know where to listen!

Why Do Angel Numbers appear to us?

Life can be a wild ride, sometimes thrilling, sometimes terrifying, and often leaving us feeling like we're navigating a blind maze. It's in these moments of uncertainty that the whispers of the universe, disguised as angel numbers, come floating into our lives. These repeating sequences, like 11:11 on your clock or 444 on your receipt, aren't just coincidences they're celestial nudges, gentle reassurances from your angels or spirit guides.

Think of them as cosmic Morse code, messages of support and encouragement beamed down just for you. When you're facing a tough decision, these numbers might appear as a comforting 777, reminding you to trust your gut and step bravely into the unknown. Feeling lost and adrift? A string of 333s could be a divine pat on the back, whispering, "You're exactly where you need to be, keep going." They're celestial cheerleaders, reminding you that even in the darkest moments, you're never alone.

But angel numbers aren't just sunshine and rainbows. They can also act as cosmic wake-up calls, a series of 222s flashing by as a warning to slow down and pay attention, or 000s urging you to release the past and embrace new beginnings. They're gentle guides, helping you navigate the twists and turns of your path, sometimes with a reassuring hug, sometimes with a firm but necessary nudge.

The key is to tune in. When those numbers catch your eye, take a moment to quiet your mind and listen to your intuition. What were you thinking about just then? What's going on in your life? The answers lie hidden within the emotions these numbers evoke. Think of it like deciphering a secret language, only the dictionary is your own heart.

How to Use Angel Numbers in your Life:

The world hums with hidden messages, whispers woven into the fabric of our daily lives. And sometimes, those whispers come in the form of repeating numbers – angel numbers, some call them. These can be repeating patterns like checking your phone at 4:34 and then seeing $4.34 on your coffee receipt. Or it can be repeating numbers or sequences like 11:11 on the clock or 1234 on a license plate. These aren't just random coincidences. They're celestial nudges, little messages from your angels or spirit guides, meant to guide, inspire, and maybe even give you a cosmic high five.

But how do you turn these number whispers into personal epiphanies? Here's your guide to unlocking the magic of angel numbers in your life:

Step one: Tune in. Keep your eyes peeled for those repeating sequences. They could be hiding anywhere – on clocks, receipts, license plates, even in your dreams. Remember, the universe loves playing hide-and-seek with its wisdom.

Step two: Crack the code. Once you've spotted a sequence, grab this book and dive into the hidden meanings. 111 might be a cosmic "go for it!" for your new adventure, while 222 could be a gentle reminder to find harmony in your relationships. Each number holds a unique story, waiting to be discovered.

Step three: Context is king. The meaning of an angel number isn't just about the number itself, but also about the situation you're in. Seeing 555 after a big breakup might mean it's time to let go and embrace new beginnings, while

777 flashing on your screen before a big presentation could be a cosmic good luck charm.

Step four: Trust your gut. Sometimes, the angels speak to your intuition, not your head. So, when you see a number sequence, pay attention to how it makes you feel. Does it spark excitement? A sense of calm? Listen to that inner voice – it's often the loudest whisper of all.

Step five: Let them guide you. Angel numbers aren't just fortune cookies; they're powerful tools for growth and transformation. Use their insights to make decisions, overcome challenges, and manifest your dreams. Remember, the universe is cheering you on every step of the way.

Finally, remember: The world of angel numbers is a personal journey. Some may see them everywhere, while others might encounter them more sporadically. But the key is to be open to their magic, to listen to the whispers, and to let them guide you on your unique and wondrous path. After all, the universe speaks in mysterious ways, and sometimes, the answers we seek are hidden in plain sight, disguised as a simple sequence of numbers, just waiting to be discovered.

As you become more attuned to this secret language, you'll find the world around you buzzing with hidden messages. Angel numbers become not just fleeting coincidences, but powerful tools for personal growth, inspiration, and guidance. So keep your eyes peeled, your heart open, and your intuition on high alert. The universe is speaking, and with a little code-cracking and trust, you'll discover that your angels are always just a whisper away, ready to guide you on your most wondrous journey yet.

Additional Tips for Unlocking your Divine Messages:

Tuning into the whispers of angels through numbers can be a beautiful way to navigate life's currents. To deepen your connection with these divine messages, here are some handy tips:

Journaling your encounters: Think of your journal as a celestial diary. Jot down the number sequences you spot and your intuitive interpretations. Over time, patterns may emerge, whispering hidden truths and nudging you towards deeper understanding.

Meditative musing: When a number sequence lingers in your mind, carve out some quiet time. Sit comfortably, close your eyes, and let the number's essence wash over you. Feel its vibrations, contemplate its meaning, and allow your inner wisdom to whisper its guidance.

Sharing the celestial messages: Discussing your angelic encounters with others can be a harmonizing experience. By sharing your observations and interpretations, you can gain fresh perspectives and weave a richer tapestry of meaning. Remember, sometimes, the most profound insights spark from unexpected conversations.

Deciphering the longer number sequences: Don't fret if you encounter an angel number sequence with four or more digits. Your trusty guidebook can still be your celestial compass. Simply break down the number into smaller units of two or three digits, like magical musical phrases. Look up their meanings in the book, and listen closely to the combined melody they create.

Whispers along the journey: As you navigate life's winding paths, you might notice similar number sequences popping up, especially when you're nearing a milestone or facing a choice. Don't underestimate these subtle nudges! Even small shifts in your journey can resonate deeply with the universe, and these repeated sequences are like celestial high-fives, acknowledging your progress and encouraging you to keep moving forward.

Remember, angel numbers are a personal language, spoken in the whispers of your intuition. How you choose to interpret and use them is entirely up to you. Be open to their guidance, let them light your path, and watch your life transform into a symphony of joy and fulfillment.

Angel Number 0

Ah, angel number 0! This seemingly small number actually packs a big punch in the realm of angelic messages. It symbolizes potential, beginnings, infinite possibilities, and a connection to the divine. While it can sometimes appear alongside other angel numbers to amplify their energies, seeing 0 by itself signifies a potent moment of transition, new starts, and an open field of potential waiting to be explored. Seeing this number repeatedly is a powerful sign from your angels that exciting possibilities await you. Here's a closer look at what angel number 0 might mean for you:

Embracing New Beginnings:

Fresh Start: 0 is a sign that a cycle is ending and a new one is about to begin. This could be anything from a new job or relationship to a shift in your perspective or life direction. Be open to possibilities and embrace the blank slate!

Planting Seeds: Think of this as the moment you plant the seeds of your future. What intentions do you want to set?

What dreams do you want to nurture? 0 encourages you to focus on your desires and start taking action toward them.

Infinite Potential: There are no limits to what you can achieve with 0 on your side. This is a reminder of your inherent power and capacity for growth. Believe in yourself and your ability to create the life you want.

Connecting with the Divine:

Spiritual awakening: 0 can indicate a deepening connection to your spirituality. It is a reminder that you are part of something greater than yourself and that you are guided by unseen forces. Pay attention to your intuition and seek guidance from higher sources.

Oneness with everything: 0 symbolizes the interconnectedness of all things. It encourages you to break down barriers and see the unity in everything around you. Practice compassion, understanding, and love towards yourself and others.

Inner peace and wholeness: This number can also be a reminder of your inherent wholeness and oneness with all that is. Let go of anxieties and embrace a sense of inner peace and acceptance.

Additional Themes:

Cycles and endings: Sometimes 0 can indicate the completion of a phase or cycle in your life. Don't resist the ending, but see it as a necessary step towards new beginnings.

Intuition and inner guidance: Pay attention to your gut feelings and inner whispers. 0 encourages you to trust your intuition and let it guide your decisions.

Release and surrender: Letting go of outdated beliefs, fears, and limitations can pave the way for new growth. Be willing to release what no longer serves you and embrace the unknown.

Oneness and wholeness: Angel number 0 represents the concept of oneness and wholeness. Everything is interconnected, and you are part of something much bigger than yourself.

Amplification: When appearing with other numbers, angel number 0 can amplify their energy and significance. Pay attention to the numbers surrounding it for deeper insights.

Here are some questions to ponder when you see angel number 0:

- What areas of your life feel stuck or ready for a new beginning?
- Are there any limiting beliefs holding you back from your potential?
- What message do you feel like the universe is sending you through this number?
- How can you strengthen your connection to your spirituality and intuition?
- Are there any negative thoughts or patterns you need to release?

- What new possibilities or goals are you ready to manifest?

Remember:

- Seeing angel number 0 is a positive sign that your angels are encouraging you to embrace your limitless potential, welcome new beginnings, and deepen your spiritual connection.
- Don't be afraid to step outside your comfort zone and explore new possibilities. Trust your intuition and let the universe guide you.
- Remember, you are one with everything, and you are capable of achieving anything you set your mind to..
- Embrace the new beginnings, explore your spiritual connection, and focus on manifesting your desires.
- Stay positive, take action, and trust the unfolding of your life path.

Angel Number 1

The angel number 1 vibrates with positive energy and holds powerful messages of new beginnings, fresh starts, and amazing opportunities.

It's often seen as a sign from your guardian angels that new opportunities and exciting possibilities are on the horizon. Here's a breakdown of its key meanings:

Embrace Fresh Starts and New Beginnings:

Close old chapters: This number encourages you to let go of anything holding you back, whether it's limiting beliefs, past relationships, or stagnant situations. Make space for new possibilities and exciting adventures.

Plant new seeds: It's time to initiate new projects, pursue your passions, and set your sights on fresh goals. Don't be afraid to take calculated risks and step outside your comfort zone.

Embrace the pioneer spirit: Angel number 1 encourages you to be a trailblazer, an innovator, and a leader in your own right. Trust your intuition and carve your own unique path.

Embrace Independence and Self-Leadership:

Believe in your own power: Angel number 1 reminds you that you are capable of achieving anything you set your mind to. Trust your abilities and take charge of your life.

Develop your assertiveness: Learn to communicate your needs and desires clearly and confidently. Don't be afraid to stand up for yourself and make decisions that align with your values.

Embrace your individuality: This number encourages you to celebrate your unique strengths, talents, and perspectives. Don't be afraid to stand out from the crowd and be true to yourself.

Additional Themes of Angel Number 1:

Motivation and inspiration: Angel number 1 can also be a sign of increased motivation and inspiration. Use this energy to take action and pursue your dreams with renewed enthusiasm.

Positive change and transformation: This encourages you to embrace positive change and transformation. See challenges as opportunities for growth and expansion.

Love and Relationships: In love, angel number 1 can symbolize the start of a new romance, a fresh chapter in an existing relationship, or the need to take initiative and express your feelings.

Career and Finances: In your career, this number can signify new opportunities, promotions, or successful ventures. In finances, it can indicate abundance and prosperity.

Spirituality: Angel number 1 can be a sign of spiritual awakening or growth. It encourages you to connect with your higher self and your purpose in life.

How to Embrace Angel Number 1:

- Be open to new beginnings and opportunities.
- Trust your intuition and follow your own path.
- Stay positive and focused on your goals.
- Take action and make things happen.
- Be grateful for the blessings in your life.

Remember: The specific meaning of angel number 1 for you will depend on your individual circumstances and what's going on in your life at the moment. Pay attention to the context in which you see the number and how it makes you feel.

Here are some questions to ask yourself:

- What have you been thinking or feeling lately?
- Are you at a crossroads in your life?
- Are you considering making a change?
- What are your hopes and dreams for the future?
- What area of your life feels stagnant or ready for change?
- What new ventures or dreams have been stirring within you?
- What limiting beliefs or fears are holding you back?

- How can you take a step forward towards your goals with courage and enthusiasm?

Remember:

- Seeing angel number 1 is a positive sign that your angels are encouraging you to embrace new beginnings, take action, and step into your power.
- Believe in yourself, trust your intuition, and be the leader of your own life.
- Embrace fresh starts, cultivate independence, and inspire others with your unique spirit.
- Stay positive and open to new possibilities.

Angel Number 2

Ah, the gentle and powerful number 2! Seeing this angel number is often a sign of balance, harmony, and partnership coming your way. Here's a breakdown of its key meanings and what you can do when it appears:

Embrace Balance, Harmony, and Connection:

Seek equilibrium in all aspects: Angel number 2 encourages you to find balance in your physical, emotional, mental, and spiritual well-being. Prioritize self-care, healthy relationships, and activities that bring you peace and joy.

Nurture your relationships: Strengthen your bonds with loved ones, practice active listening and empathy, and offer support and understanding. Remember, true connection thrives on balance and reciprocity.

Seek peaceful solutions: When faced with challenges, approach them with a calm and collaborative spirit. Look for win-win solutions and prioritize understanding over conflict.

Embrace Love and Service:

Open your heart to love: Angel number 2 reminds you that love is abundant and available to you. Expand your capacity for love, both for yourself and others.

Express your love freely: Show your loved ones how much they mean to you through words, actions, and gestures of kindness. Be open to receiving love in return.

Serve others with compassion: Use your talents and gifts to make a positive impact on the world around you. Consider volunteering your time, sharing your knowledge, or simply offering a listening ear.

Additional Themes of Angel Number 2:

Home and family: Angel number 2 can also signify the importance of home and family life. Cultivate a warm and harmonious environment for yourself and loved ones.

Healing and forgiveness: This number can also encourage you to let go of past hurts and forgive yourself and others. Healing allows you to move forward with peace and clarity.

Material abundance: Angel number 2 can also signify abundance in material and emotional aspects of life. Trust that you have everything you need and are worthy of receiving more.

Partnership and collaboration: This number can also encourage you to seek partnerships and work collaboratively towards shared goals. Remember, teamwork makes the dream work!

Intuition and diplomacy: Angel number 2 encourages you to tap into your intuitive wisdom and navigate situations with diplomacy and grace.

Faith and trust: This number can also be a reminder to have faith in the universe and trust that everything is unfolding as it should.

Here are some questions to ask yourself:

- Where in my life is there an imbalance I need to address? (Work-life balance, emotional well-being, etc.)
- How can I nurture more peace and harmony in my relationships?
- What are my deepest passions and talents that I feel called to share?
- Am I open to receiving guidance and collaborating with others on my journey?
- Do I fully trust my own intuition and inner wisdom?
- Where am I holding onto doubts or fears that need to be released?

What to Do When You See Angel Number 2:

- Seek balance: Take a step back and assess where you need to find equilibrium. Is it your workload, your relationships, or your internal state?
- Nurture your partnerships: Invest time and energy in your relationships, both personal and professional. Communicate openly and work towards common goals.

- Trust your intuition: Pay attention to your gut feelings and inner voice. They can guide you towards the right decisions and opportunities.
- Open your heart to love: Be receptive to new connections and deepen existing ones. Express your love and appreciation for those around you.
- Practice diplomacy and peacemaking: Seek solutions that benefit everyone and strive for harmony in your interactions.

Remember:

- Seeing angel number 2 is a positive sign that you are on the right path. It's a reminder to cultivate balance, nurture relationships, and trust your inner guidance.
- Embrace the opportunities for cooperation, love, and harmony that come your way.
- With a balanced approach and an open heart, you can navigate life's challenges and create a fulfilling journey for yourself.
- Trust your intuition, collaborate with others, and cultivate faith in yourself and the universe.
- Embrace the journey of personal growth and remember that you are never alone.

Angel Number 3

Angel number 3 vibrates with positive energy and carries powerful messages of growth, creativity, communication, and optimism. Seeing this number is a sign from your angels that they are with you, supporting you on your journey towards self-expression, joy, and manifestation. Here's a breakdown of what angel number 3 might mean for you:

Embrace Creativity and Self-Expression:

Explore your artistic side: Whether it's writing, painting, music, or anything else that sparks your joy, unleash your creative energy and share your unique gifts with the world.

Express yourself authentically: Don't be afraid to let your voice be heard and share your true thoughts and feelings. Speak your truth and embrace your individuality.

Connect with your inner child: Allow yourself to play, have fun, and explore new possibilities with an open and curious mind.

Embrace Growth and Expansion:

Step into your power: Angel number 3 encourages you to believe in yourself and your abilities. Take risks, pursue your passions, and don't be afraid to step outside your comfort zone.

Embrace new experiences: Open yourself to learning and personal growth. Explore new hobbies, travel to new places, and connect with different people. Expansion awaits you!

Develop your talents: Angel number 3 often appears when you are called to share your unique gifts with the world. Hone your skills, express your creativity, and let your light shine.

Enhance Communication and Connection:

Speak your truth: Express yourself authentically and openly. Don't be afraid to share your thoughts, feelings, and ideas with the world.

Listen with empathy: Pay attention to others, offer support, and practice active listening. Strong communication builds bridges and strengthens connections.

Collaborate and connect: Angel number 3 encourages teamwork and collaboration. Seek out partnerships, join groups, and work towards shared goals.

Cultivate Optimism and Joy:

Focus on the positive: Choose to see the good in every situation, even when faced with challenges. Maintain a positive outlook and believe in the power of hope.

Celebrate your successes: Acknowledge your accomplishments, big and small. Share your joy with others and let yourself bask in the feeling of achievement.

Embrace playfulness and joy: Angel number 3 reminds you to enjoy life's simple pleasures. Make time for laughter, fun activities, and things that bring you joy.

Embrace Manifestation:

Focus on your desires and visualize your goals: The power of your thoughts and intentions is strong. Clearly define your dreams and hold them in your mind's eye with strong belief.

Take inspired action: Don't just dream, take concrete steps towards your goals. Align your actions with your intentions and actively work towards bringing your desires into reality.

Trust the universe and the timing of your manifestations: Your dreams may unfold in unexpected ways, so stay open to receiving blessings in different forms and timings.

Here are some key questions to ponder that can help you unlock the specific message your angels are sending when you see the number 3:

- Am I neglecting my creative side or passions? What can I do to express myself more authentically?
- Do I hold any limiting beliefs about my talents or voice that need to be released?
- How can I connect with my inner child and infuse more playfulness and joy into my daily life?
- What areas of my life feel stagnant or ready for expansion? Where can I learn new things or broaden my horizons?

- Am I listening to my intuition and taking inspired action towards my goals and dreams?
- Am I living with passion and enthusiasm, or do I need to rekindle my internal spark?
- Am I clearly visualizing my dreams and holding them in my mind with strong belief?

Remember:

- Seeing angel number 3 is a positive and encouraging sign that your angels are with you, supporting your creative endeavors, personal growth, and joyful journey.
- Embrace your unique spark, expand your horizons, cultivate joy, and believe in your ability to manifest your dreams.
- Trust your intuition, take inspired action, and keep radiating your light!
- Embrace new experiences, express yourself creatively, and communicate openly.
- Cultivate optimism, celebrate your successes, and find joy in the journey.

Angel Number 4

The angel number 4 resonates with stability, groundedness, practicality, and hard work. Seeing this number repeatedly is a sign from your angels that they are encouraging you to build a solid foundation in your life, work diligently towards your goals, and remain focused on achievement. Here's how angel number 4 might be guiding you:

Embrace Stability and Groundedness:

Seek balance in all areas of your life: This includes your physical, emotional, mental, and spiritual well-being. Prioritize self-care, healthy habits, and activities that bring you a sense of calm and security.

Develop strong foundations: Whether it's in your career, relationships, or personal finances, focus on building a solid base that can support you in the long run.

Practice discipline and routine: Create healthy habits and routines that provide structure and stability in your daily life. Consistency and perseverance are key to achieving your goals.

Embrace Discipline and Hard Work:

Persevere through challenges: Don't be discouraged by obstacles or setbacks. Angel number 4 reminds you that hard work and dedication will ultimately lead to success.

Develop strong work ethic: Cultivate discipline, focus, and perseverance in your endeavors. Be willing to put in the effort and dedicate time to achieving your goals.

Stay organized and efficient: Implement routines and systems that help you manage your time and resources effectively. Structure and organization can support your productivity and keep you on track.

Embrace Practicality and Responsibility:

Make responsible decisions: Think carefully before making choices, and consider the potential consequences. Angel number 4 encourages wise and practical decision-making.

Fulfill your commitments: Be reliable and trustworthy, and follow through on your promises. Take ownership of your responsibilities and actions.

Focus on long-term goals: Don't get caught up in short-term distractions or quick fixes. Angel number 4 encourages a long-term perspective and building a sustainable future.

Remember:

- Seeing angel number 4 is a positive sign that your angels are with you, supporting you on your journey towards stability, achievement, and solid foundations.

- Number 4 is not a sign to give up or slow down, but rather to approach your goals with focus, discipline, and a practical mindset.
- Trust your abilities to build a stable and secure future for yourself. Your hard work and dedication will pay off in the long run.
- Embrace responsibility, hard work, and perseverance, and don't be afraid to put in the effort to achieve your goals.
- Stay grounded in your values and priorities, and don't be afraid to make necessary changes to create a life you truly desire.
- Build a strong foundation in your life, set realistic goals, and always strive for excellence.
- Trust the process, stay focused, and don't give up on your dreams.

Seeing angel number 4 is a nudge to delve deeper into your foundation, work ethic, and sense of responsibility. Here are some questions to guide your self-reflection:

- Where in my life do I need to focus on building more stability or grounding?
- Am I setting realistic and achievable goals for myself?
- Am I putting in the necessary effort to achieve my desired outcomes?
- Are there any limiting beliefs or fears that are holding me back from reaching my full potential?
- Am I putting in the necessary effort to achieve my goals? What challenges am I avoiding?
- How can I develop more discipline and commitment in my everyday life?

- Am I taking full ownership of my actions and choices? Are there any areas where I need to hold myself more accountable?

By reflecting on these questions and taking action according to your insights, you can unlock the full potential of angel number 4 and create a life of stability, success, and grounded achievement.

Angel Number 5

Angel number 5 vibrates with the energy of positive change, adaptability, freedom, and adventure. Seeing this number repeatedly is a sign from your angels that exciting transformations are on the horizon, urging you to embrace new opportunities, let go of limitations, and pursue your passions with enthusiasm. Here's a breakdown of what angel number 5 might mean for you:

Embrace Change and New Beginnings:

Be open to fresh perspectives and exciting opportunities: Change, despite its potential discomfort, can lead to immense growth and fulfillment. Embrace new chapters in your life, whether it's a career shift, a relocation, or a change in relationships.

Release the past and let go of what no longer serves you: Don't cling to outdated patterns or stagnant situations. Acknowledge what needs to be released and open yourself to the influx of fresh energy and new possibilities.

Step outside your comfort zone: Don't be afraid to take risks and venture into the unknown. Challenges and unfamiliar territories can often lead to the most rewarding experiences and personal breakthroughs.

Embrace Adventure and Freedom:

Infuse your life with spontaneity and excitement: Seek out new experiences, travel to unfamiliar places, and indulge in activities that spark your adventurous spirit. Break free from routines and embrace the thrill of exploring and discovering.

Live with an open heart and a free spirit: Don't let fear or expectations confine you. Embrace individuality, express your authentic self, and live life on your own terms.

Listen to your inner voice and follow your passions: Pursue what excites you and makes you feel truly alive. Don't be afraid to break free from societal pressures and chase your unique dreams and desires.

Embrace Adaptability and Resourcefulness:

Be open to new approaches and flexible in your thinking: Change is inevitable, so learn to adapt to different situations and embrace challenges as opportunities to learn and grow.

Trust your intuition and resourcefulness: You have everything you need within you to navigate any situation or overcome any obstacle. Trust your inner wisdom and your ability to find creative solutions.

Embrace diversity and learn from others: Expand your horizons by exposing yourself to different cultures, perspectives, and ways of life. Openness and adaptability will enrich your experiences and empower you to face anything life throws your way.

Seeing angel number 5 is a delightful nudge to explore themes of positive change, adaptability, and embracing new adventures. Here are some questions to guide your self-reflection when you encounter this powerful number:

- What areas of my life feel stagnant or ready for a fresh start? What changes might be on the horizon?
- Are there any limiting beliefs or fears holding me back from embracing these changes? How can I release them?
- Am I living a life true to my passions and desires? Where can I add more freedom and spontaneity to my routine?
- What are some risks I've been wanting to take but haven't yet? What is holding me back, and how can I overcome it?
- Am I open to unexpected opportunities and unplanned adventures? How can I cultivate a more adventurous spirit?
- Am I neglecting my sensuality and enjoyment of life's simple pleasures? How can I cultivate a more balanced and joyful approach to my life?

Remember:

- Seeing angel number 5 is a positive sign that your angels are cheering you on as you embark on a journey of change, adventure, and personal liberation.
- Stay open-minded, adaptable, and true to yourself. Trust your intuition, take inspired action, and enjoy the exciting ride!

- Embrace change, step outside your comfort zone, and trust your intuition to guide you towards exciting new experiences.
- Celebrate your individuality, break free from limitations, and discover the joy of living life on your own terms.
- Trust your intuition, adapt to new situations, and enjoy the journey of growth and expansion that awaits you.

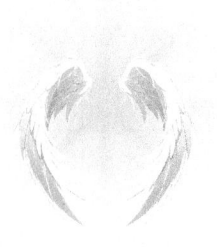

Angel Number 6

Angel number 6! This vibrant number radiates the energy of balance, harmony, responsibility, love, and nurturing. Seeing this number repeatedly is a sign from your angels encouraging you to cultivate a balanced life, nurture your relationships, embrace responsibility with grace, and spread love in all its forms. Here's how angel number 6 might be guiding you:

Embrace Balance and Harmony:

Seek equilibrium in all aspects of your life: This includes your physical, emotional, mental, and spiritual well-being. Prioritize self-care, healthy relationships, and activities that bring you joy and peace.

Seek win-win solutions: When faced with challenges, approach them with a collaborative spirit and seek solutions that benefit everyone involved. Remember, balance often lies in understanding different perspectives.

Nurture your connection to nature: Spend time in nature to find your center and reconnect with the harmony of the universe. Nature's beauty and balance can offer insights for finding balance within yourself.

Embrace Responsibility and Service:

Fulfill your commitments and obligations: Angel number 6 reminds you to be reliable, trustworthy, and accountable for your actions. Take responsibility for your choices and contribute meaningfully to your community.

Offer your gifts and talents to others: Use your skills and knowledge to support those around you and make a positive impact on the world. Service brings personal fulfillment and strengthens your connection to others.

Lead with integrity and compassion: Make decisions based on your values and treat everyone with respect. Your strong moral compass inspires others to do the same.

Embrace Love and Nurturing:

Open your heart to love in all its forms: This includes romantic love, family love, friendships, and love for yourself. Cultivate kindness, empathy, and understanding in your relationships.

Express your love and appreciation: Don't be afraid to tell your loved ones how much they mean to you. Small gestures of kindness and compassion can have a profound impact on others.

Nurture your creativity and inner child: Angel number 6 encourages you to explore your artistic side and find joy in simple pleasures. Playfulness and creativity can bring joy and balance to your life.

Additional Themes:

Home and family: Angel number 6 can also signify a focus on strengthening your home life and family bonds. Prioritize quality time with loved ones and create a nurturing environment.

Financial responsibility: This number can also encourage responsible financial management. Make wise choices, cultivate abundance, and avoid relying on others for support.

Compassion and forgiveness: Angel number 6 reminds you to treat yourself and others with compassion. Forgive yourself and others for past mistakes and focus on moving forward with kindness.

Seeing angel number 6 is a beautiful invitation to delve deeper into the themes of balance, love, and service. Here are some questions to guide your self-reflection as you encounter this potent number:

- Where in my life is there an imbalance I need to address? (Work-life balance, emotional well-being, etc.)
- How can I nurture more peace and harmony in my relationships?
- Am I approaching challenges with a collaborative spirit or seeking win-win solutions?
- Am I open to receiving and expressing love freely in my life?
- How can I better connect with loved ones and strengthen my existing relationships?
- Am I taking full ownership of my actions and choices?
- Are there any commitments I need to prioritize or follow through on?

- How can I become a more dependable and supportive friend, family member, or partner?

Remember:

- Seeing angel number 6 is a positive and encouraging sign that your angels are supporting you on your journey to create a balanced, harmonious, and loving life.
- Embrace responsibility, nurture your relationships, and spread love in all its forms.
- Trust your intuition, collaborate with others, and remember that true balance lies in the heart of everything you do.
- Take responsibility for your actions, contribute your talents to the world, and be a reliable and trustworthy presence.
- Trust the process, stay open to change, and embrace the beautiful journey of balance, love, and service that awaits you.

Angel Number 7

Angel number 7 vibrates with the powerful energy of spiritual growth, introspection, wisdom, and intuition. Seeing this number repeatedly is a sign from your angels that they're encouraging you to deepen your connection to your inner self, embrace self-discovery, and trust your inner guidance. Here's a breakdown of what angel number 7 might mean for you:

Embrace Spiritual Growth and Introspection:

Seek deeper understanding: Angel number 7 encourages you to delve into your spiritual life, explore your beliefs, and connect with your higher purpose. This may involve meditation, prayer, studying sacred texts, or simply spending time in quiet reflection.

Embrace solitude and introspection: Take time for yourself, away from the noise and distractions of everyday life. Use this space to listen to your inner voice, reflect on your experiences, and gain insights into your true desires and goals.

Develop your intuition: Trust your gut feelings and inner wisdom. Pay attention to recurring thoughts, dreams, and synchronicities, as they may hold messages from your angels or your subconscious.

Embrace Wisdom and Knowledge:

Seek knowledge and understanding: This may involve formal education, self-study, or simply being open to learning from your experiences and the people around you. Wisdom comes from a combination of knowledge and experience.

Share your wisdom with others: Don't be afraid to share your insights and knowledge with others. By teaching and guiding others, you deepen your own understanding and make a positive contribution to the world.

Embrace critical thinking: Develop your ability to analyze situations objectively and make informed decisions. Don't be afraid to challenge your own beliefs and question the status quo.

Embrace Intuition and Inner Guidance:

Trust your gut feeling: When faced with a decision, listen to your inner voice. Your intuition often knows the right path before you consciously do.

Be open to receiving guidance: Your angels and spirit guides are always with you, offering support and guidance. Be open to receiving their messages through dreams, intuition, or synchronicities.

Take action based on your intuition: Don't be afraid to take risks and follow your inner guidance, even if it seems unconventional. True growth often happens outside your comfort zone.

Additional Themes:

Luck and good fortune: Though not its core meaning, Angel number 7 is often associated with luck and good fortune. Trust that the universe is supporting you on your journey and allow yourself to receive unexpected blessings.

Second chances and learning from mistakes: This number can also signify new beginnings and opportunities for second chances. Learn from your past mistakes and move forward with newfound wisdom.

Empathy and compassion: Angel number 7 encourages you to develop your empathy and compassion for yourself and others. Be kind, understanding, and supportive towards yourself and those around you.

When you encounter the potent energy of angel number 7, it's an invitation to dive deeper into your spiritual journey and inner wisdom. Here are some questions to guide your self-reflection as you contemplate its meaning:

- Have I been neglecting my spiritual needs or inner world lately? What practices can I incorporate to foster deeper connection and introspection?
- How can I better listen to and trust my intuition? Are there recurring voices or gut feelings I've been ignoring?

- What areas of knowledge are calling to me right now? What can I learn or study to grow and expand my horizons?
- How can I use my existing knowledge and wisdom to empower and inspire others? What gifts can I share with the world?
- Are there any recurring fears, doubts, or limiting beliefs I need to address and release to access my true potential?
- What spiritual practices or teachings resonate with me and could help me deepen my connection to the universe?

Remember:

- Seeing angel number 7 is a positive sign that your angels are supporting you on your journey of spiritual growth, self-discovery, and trusting your inner guidance.
- Embrace your intuition, dive deep into introspection, and trust your unique path.
- Be open to learning, grow from your experiences, and express your soul's desires through your individual gifts.
- Trust the universe, allow yourself to receive blessings, and radiate your inner light to the world.
- Embrace introspection, seek wisdom, and trust your intuition.
- Take time for yourself, develop your spiritual connection, and follow your inner compass.
- Believe in your potential, embrace challenges as opportunities for growth, and know that you are on the right path.

Angel Number 8

Angel number 8 resonates with powerful energy of abundance, infinity, transformation, personal power, and manifestation. Seeing this number repeatedly is a sign from your angels that you are entering a period of immense growth, prosperity, and achieving your goals. Here's a breakdown of what angel number 8 might mean for you:

Embrace Abundance and Prosperity:

Believe in your inherent abundance: You are worthy of receiving and enjoying all forms of abundance, both material and spiritual. Trust that the universe is providing for you.

Focus on gratitude and appreciation: Acknowledge the blessings you already have in your life, big and small. Gratitude attracts more abundance and opens you to receiving even more.

Take inspired action: Manifestation requires action. Align your thoughts and desires with concrete steps and work towards your goals with determination and focus.

Embrace Transformation and Personal Power:

Be open to change and growth: Angel number 8 encourages you to step outside your comfort zone and embrace new challenges. These experiences will help you evolve and reach your full potential.

Develop your inner strength and confidence: Believe in yourself and your ability to overcome any obstacle. Trust your intuition and take ownership of your choices and actions.

Break free from limiting beliefs: Identify any negative thoughts or self-doubt that hold you back from achieving your dreams. Release these limiting beliefs and replace them with positive affirmations and self-compassion.

Additional Themes of Angel Number 8:

Karma and cause-and-effect: Angel number 8 reminds you that your actions have consequences. Choose your words and actions wisely, as they will ripple outwards and affect your future.

Balance and justice: This number also encourages you to strive for balance in all aspects of your life. Be fair, just, and compassionate in your interactions with others.

Leadership and service: Angel number 8 can also suggest that you have leadership qualities and are destined to guide and inspire others. Use your talents and skills to make a positive impact on the world.

Seeing angel number 8 is a vibrant invitation to delve deeper into themes of abundance, personal power, and transformation. Here are some questions to guide your self-reflection when you encounter this potent number:

- Where in my life do I desire more abundance? (Finances, love, creativity, etc.)
- What limiting beliefs might I be holding about receiving abundance?
- How can I cultivate a more positive mindset and practice gratitude for what I already have?
- What specific goals or desires can I clearly define and focus on manifesting?
- What are my unique strengths, talents, and abilities that I can tap into and develop further?
- Are there any areas in my life where I feel powerless or stuck? What steps can I take to reclaim my power and move forward?
- How can I embrace positive change and view it as an opportunity for growth and expansion?

Remember:

- Seeing angel number 8 is a positive and encouraging sign that your angels are supporting you on your journey to abundance, transformation, and personal power.
- Embrace the changes coming your way, believe in your ability to manifest your desires, and take action towards your goals.

- Develop your inner strength, release limiting beliefs, and strive for balance and justice in your life.
- Use your talents and skills to make a positive impact on the world and inspire others.
- Believe in your own power, practice gratitude, and release limiting beliefs to open yourself to greater possibilities.
- Be aware of the karmic cycle and focus on creating positive energy in your life.

Angel Number 9

Angel number 9 resonates with the powerful energies of completion, endings, new beginnings, compassion, and humanitarianism. Seeing this number repeatedly is a sign from your angels that a significant chapter in your life is coming to a close, paving the way for fresh starts and new opportunities. Here's a breakdown of what angel number 9 might mean for you:

Embrace Completion and Letting Go:

Acknowledge endings: Recognize and accept the closing of a cycle, whether it be a relationship, career phase, or personal project. Release what no longer serves you and make space for new beginnings.

Let go of attachments: This doesn't mean forgetting, but releasing unhealthy attachments to past experiences or outcomes. Forgive yourself and others, and move forward with a clean slate.

Trust the divine timing: Angel number 9 reminds you that endings are not failures, but necessary steps in your journey. Trust that the timing of these transitions is divinely orchestrated for your highest good.

Embrace New Beginnings and Fresh Starts:

Open yourself to new possibilities: As one door closes, another opens. Be receptive to new opportunities and experiences that may arise from the ending you're experiencing.

Embrace your creative potential: This is a time for renewal and fresh starts. Pursue your passions, explore new avenues, and tap into your creative energy.

Plant seeds for the future: Focus on setting intentions and taking action towards your goals for the next chapter. The seeds you plant now will blossom in the future.

Embrace Compassion and Service:

Develop your sense of empathy: Angel number 9 encourages you to connect with others on a deeper level, offer support, and act with compassion.

Use your gifts to serve others: Consider how you can use your talents and skills to make a positive impact on the world around you. Volunteer your time, donate to causes you care about, or simply offer a helping hand to those in need.

Embrace a global perspective: Angel number 9 can also nudge you to connect with the larger human family and consider how your actions can contribute to a better world for all.

Additional Themes:

Karma and karmic cycles: Angel number 9 can sometimes signify the completion of karmic cycles and reaping the rewards or facing the consequences of past actions.

Spiritual growth and enlightenment: This number can also guide you on your journey of spiritual awakening and connection to something greater than yourself.

Letting go of ego and materialism: Angel number 9 encourages you to focus on inner values and let go of attachments to material possessions.

When you see the vibrant number 9, it's an invitation to delve deeper into themes of completion, new beginnings, and using your gifts for the greater good. Here are some questions to guide your self-reflection:

- What areas of my life feel like they are nearing completion? Am I ready to let go and embrace new possibilities?
- Are there any limiting beliefs or attachments holding me back from moving forward? How can I release them?
- What excites me about the future? What new opportunities am I open to?
- How can I use my unique talents and gifts to make a positive impact on the world? What is my soul's calling?
- Am I cultivating compassion and understanding towards myself and others? How can I extend more support and service?

- In what ways can I become a beacon of hope and inspiration for others?

Remember:

- Seeing angel number 9 is a positive sign that your angels are supporting you through transitions and preparing you for new beginnings.
- Embrace the process of endings and new starts, let go of what no longer serves you, and open yourself to the exciting possibilities that await.
- Cultivate compassion, serve others, and connect to your higher purpose for a fulfilling and meaningful life.
- Trust your intuition, express yourself creatively, and deepen your spiritual connection.
- Remember the karmic cycle and practice forgiveness to move forward with peace and clarity.

Angel Numbers

1: It's time for a fresh start! Take the lead, trust your gut, and paint your own masterpiece.

2: Feeling pulled in two directions? Breathe, find balance. Harmony with others and within is your superpower.

3: Unleash your inner artist! Sing, paint, write – your creative spark is a beacon in the world. Shine it bright!

4: Steady as you go. Hard work and dedication lay the foundation for a rock-solid future.

5: Adventure awaits! Break free from the routine, embrace new experiences, and let your wings fly.

6: Open your heart, nurturer. Love and compassion are your gifts – share them with the world.

7: Listen to the whispers within. Your intuition is a compass guiding you to inner wisdom.

8: Angels are telling you abundance flows your way! Believe in yourself, tap into your potential, and claim your rightful prosperity.

9: Let go, it's time for a new chapter. Endings are just new beginnings in disguise. Trust the universe, new horizons await.

10: Dream big! This is a new era, brimming with potential. Focus, manifest, and watch your grand vision take flight.

11: Your inner voice echoes the cosmos! Trust your intuition, awaken your spirit, and master your own destiny.

12: Your gifts are meant to share! Channel your creativity, serve the world, and watch your dreams manifest into reality.

13: Change is inevitable, embrace adaptability, and conquer any challenge that comes your way.

14: Love heals all wounds, friend. Open your heart, offer compassion, and let this warmth mend and support you.

15: The universe is sending a message that love and relationships are ready for a makeover. Believe in new beginnings, open your heart, and watch connections blossom.

16: Release the fear, grab the goodies! Abundance is yours for the taking. Focus on the positive, let go of materialism, and watch prosperity blossom.

17: Get ready for unexpected blessings, new opportunities, and a sprinkle of serendipity. Open your arms and feel the embrace of your angels.

18: Unleash your creative beast! New beginnings in your career or artistic ventures are brewing. Spark your imagination and watch your masterpiece unfold.

19: The universe needs your big heart! Share your gifts, spread compassion, and make a difference in the world. Your service matters.

20: Take a deep breath and trust in your angels. Faith and trust will unlock inner peace. New beginnings await, so stand tall, let go, and embrace the journey.

21: Your celestial guides are telling you to see your inner light! Your intuition is a beacon, leading you to enlightenment and the wisdom within.

22: You are the architect of your own destiny! Build your dreams, manifest your desires, and unlock your boundless potential.

23: Let your voice soar on angel wings! Express yourself boldly, unleash your creativity, and let your unique song fill the world.

24: The universe is telling you to ground yourself. Embrace organization, harness practicality, and build a sturdy foundation for your dreams.

25: Break free, adventurer! Embrace change, ignite your spirit, and let your soul dance to the rhythm of freedom and spontaneity.

26: Home is where the heart blooms. Nurture your loved ones, cultivate harmony, and let love be your guiding light.

27: Seek the quiet whispers in your soul. Solitude and intuition illuminate your spiritual path, guiding you from within.

28: The angels want you to believe in your worth, claim your prosperity, and manifest your grandest dreams.

29: Open your heart. Your compassion is a gift, serve others with love, and make a difference in the world.

30: Let go, dear soul. Forgive, release, and embrace the fresh start waiting for you. New beginnings whisper on the wind, trust the cycle and open your arms to the future.

31: Let your colors explode! Inspiration ignites your soul, unleash your unique expression and paint your masterpiece on the world.

32: Your heart whispers wisdom. Serve others with intuition, spread compassion, and be the light that guides humanity forward.

33: Knowledge flows through you. Master communication, express with clarity, and inspire others to learn and grow.

34: Steady steps build empires. Embrace practicality, roll up your sleeves, and lay a solid foundation for your dreams.

35: Bend like a willow in the wind. Change is inevitable, release the old, adapt with grace, and embrace the new opportunities blossoming for you.

36: Love nourishes like sun-kissed soil. Nurture your family, embrace responsibility, and let love be the root of your strength and joy.

37: Listen to the quiet whispers within. Your intuition and inner wisdom are your compass, guiding you on your spiritual journey through solitude and self-discovery.

38: Lead with purpose, manifest with power! Abundance awaits your belief, so claim your prosperity, rise to your leadership, and make your mark on the world.

39: Shine your light! Guide others, serve with compassion, and let your humanitarian spirit make a difference in the world.

40: Close one chapter, open the next. Endings bring lessons, completion offers wisdom, and new beginnings shimmer on the horizon. Embrace the cycle, dear soul, and step boldly into the future.

41: The angels are raising you up! Time to unleash your creative spirit, take that career leap, and paint your masterpiece on the world.

42: Harmony sings sweet melodies, friend. Seek balance, nurture partnerships, and let cooperation be the bridge to your dreams.

43: Like a leaf on the wind, embrace change. Adapt with grace, let go of the past, and trust the new beginnings whispering on the breeze.

44: Angels walk beside you. Feel their support, listen to their guidance, and know you're never alone on your journey.

45: The Universe sends messages of Love! New beginnings blossom in relationships, trust your heart, and let love guide you to a deeper connection.

46: This message speaks of home. Nurture your family, embrace the warmth of your nest, and let inner peace be your guiding light.

47: Your soul whispers wisdom, listen close. Hone your spiritual gifts, trust your intuition, and let inner wisdom illuminate your path.

48: Abundance showers upon you! Believe in your worth, manifest your desires, and bask in the recognition that comes with your shining spirit.

49: Open your heart. Serve others with compassion, let go of limitations, and be the beacon of hope for humanity.

50: Angels are giving you strength! Unleash your inner power, embrace change, and embark on new adventures that will shape you into the magnificent being you are meant to be.

51: Dive deep, dear one. Trust your intuition, let inspiration ignite your spirit, and embrace the fresh start waiting for you.

Your inner voice whispers wisdom, listen closely and follow its light.

52: Harmony is the music of life, find it in every note. Seek balance, nurture collaboration, and discover your unique place within the grand orchestra of existence. Teamwork amplifies your song.

53: Let creativity flow like a vibrant river, express yourself with boldness, and share your gifts with the world. Your voice is a beacon, shine it bright and illuminate the path for others.

54: Build your dreams on a sturdy foundation, friend. Hard work and practicality are the bricks, grounding is the mortar, and a solid base ensures your aspirations reach for the sky.

55: Change is the dance of the universe, break free from routine, and let the wild spirit of new experiences guide your journey.

56: Love is the hearth of your home, let it warm your soul. Nurture your family, cultivate domestic harmony, and find peace in the embrace of those who cherish you.

57: Seek the quiet whispers of the angels. Your spiritual awakening awaits in solitude, where intuition and inner wisdom guide your steps towards enlightenment.

58: Th Cosmos speak of Abundance! Believe in your worth, manifest your desires, and use your talents for good. Let prosperity be a tool to uplift and inspire others.

59: Feel the love of your spirit guides around you. Forgive yourself and the past, let go of what no longer serves you, and make space for the new beginnings waiting to blossom.

60: Be a lightworker. Service to others is your calling, spread compassion, heal the world with your touch, and make a difference that ripples through eternity.

61: Dive into the depths of your being. Embrace your intuition, seek enlightenment, and master your connection to your higher self. You are a divine spark, remember your radiant power.

62: This message speaks of your desires. Manifest your dreams, tap into your limitless potential, and shape the world you desire with each brick of action and intention.

63: Let your voice be a beacon of wisdom. Share your knowledge, express your truth, and illuminate the path for others with your unique words of light.

64: The angels walk with you and their steady steps pave the way to success. Embrace practicality, organize your chaos, and find stability in the foundation you build. Grounding anchors your dreams, making them soar.

65: Bend like the willow in the wind, adapt with grace. The river of change flows ever onward, release the past, and embrace the new opportunities swirling around you.

66: Nurture the garden of your home, let love bloom within. Cherish your family, create a haven of harmony, and let love be the sun that warms your soul and strengthens your roots.

67: Discover your inner sanctuary. Embrace solitude, listen to your intuition, and let your spiritual journey guide you toward inner peace.

68: Claim your prosperity! Believe in your worth, achieve your financial goals, and bask in the material success that reflects your hard work and unwavering spirit.

69: Be a healer, a beacon of compassion. Serve others with open arms, spread humanitarianism like wildfire, and let your actions mend the cracks in the world.

70: Close one chapter, open the next. Embrace the lessons learned, release what no longer serves you, and step into the fresh start waiting on the horizon.

71: Unleash the wild artist within! New beginnings dance in your creative pursuits or career. Follow your passions, trust your inner fire, and paint your masterpiece on the world.

72: The angels speak of balance in all aspects of your life. Nurture cooperation and let your journey lead you to the one who resonates with your deepest melody. Your soul mate awaits, their song harmonizing with yours.

73: Embrace the wind of change. Adapt with grace, trust your intuition's compass, and let go of what no longer serves you. New opportunities bloom where flexibility takes root.

74: Angels walk beside you, whispering support and guidance. Feel their presence, trust their reassuring hand, and know you are never alone on your path. Their wings embrace you in every challenge.

75: Open your heart, beautiful soul! New beginnings blossom in love and relationships. Vulnerability is strength, embrace it, and let love paint your world with vibrant hues.

76: Nestle your spirit in a haven of peace, friend. Nurture your family, cherish home as your sanctuary, and find inner peace in the warmth of your nest. You are safe, loved, and forever held.

77: Honing your spiritual gifts is the journey within. Embrace your intuition, let inner wisdom illuminate your path, and connect with your spirit guides. They whisper guidance in the quiet moments, listen close.

78: Abundance is a reward for your unwavering spirit! Believe in your worth, manifest your desires, and bask in the recognition that reflects your achievements. You are worthy, celebrated, and radiant.

79: The universe is sending a message to release your burdens. Forgive yourself and the past, let go of what weighs you down, and make space for the abundance that awaits.

80: Rise with the strength of a mountain, claim your inner power! Confidence is your crown, wear it with pride. Take control of your life and your destiny with bold measures.

81: Dive into new beginnings, take that leap of faith, and manifest your dreams with bold action. The universe waits to witness your masterpiece.

82: Harmony is the magic of collaboration, friend. Seek balance, nurture teamwork, and find common ground. Together, you weave a symphony of success.

83: Let your voice soar, the universe is listening! Unleash your creativity, express yourself boldly, and share your unique gifts with the world. Your light illuminates the path for others.

84: Build your dreams on a bedrock of practicality. Hard work lays the foundation, and a solid base ensures your aspirations reach for the sky.

85: Embrace the dance of change, adventurer! Adapt with grace, release the past like autumn leaves, and grasp the vibrant new opportunities that swirl around you.

86: Nurture your loved ones, create a haven of support. Let love be the sun that warms your family, and build a fortress of strength together.

87: Seek the quiet whispers within, discover your inner sanctuary. Embrace your spirituality, listen to your intuition, and connect with your higher self. Wisdom awaits in the silence.

88: Abundance rains down upon you, a reward for your relentless spirit! Believe in your financial worth, manifest your prosperity, and achieve success that reflects your hard work and unwavering belief.

89: Be a lightworker, a beacon of hope. Service to others is your calling, use your gifts to make a difference, and heal the world with your compassion.

90: Close one chapter, open the next. Embrace the lessons learned, release what no longer serves you, and prepare for the new beginnings that shimmer on the horizon. The future is a canvas of endless possibilities, paint it with courage and joy.

91: Your intuition is a compass, leading you to enlightenment and mastery. Connect to your divine purpose, and let your light shine as a beacon for others.

92: Build with vision, manifest your dreams, and unleash your boundless potential. The world awaits your masterpiece, a testament to your spirit and creativity.

93: Let your voice echo through time! Share your wisdom, express your truth, and illuminate the path for others with your unique words of light. Be a teacher, a storyteller, a weaver of hope.

94: The universe whispers of grounding yourself. Embrace practicality, organize your chaos, and find stability in the foundation you build. A clear mind and steady steps fuel your ascension.

95: Dance with change, like a willow in the wind. Adapt with grace, release the past like autumn leaves, and embrace the new chapters waiting to unfold. The universe whispers fresh beginnings.

96: Nurture the garden of your heart, let love bloom within. Cherish your family, create a haven of harmony, and let love be the sun that warms your soul and strengthens your bonds.

97: Seek the quiet whispers within, discover your inner compass. In stillness, you find your true north.

98: Angels speak of a financial reward for your unwavering spirit! Believe in your worth, manifest your highest potential, and bask in the material success that reflects your achievements. You deserve prosperity, claim it with gratitude.

99: Release the burdens of your soul. Forgive yourself and the past, let go of what weighs you down, and make space for the new beginnings that shimmer on the horizon. Forgiveness is the key to unlocking abundance.

100: Embrace boundless potential. Reach for goals that seem out of reach, and watch your fire burn brightly, illuminating your path to greatness.

101: Balance flourishes in partnerships. Seek relationships where harmony thrives, communication nourishes connection, and love blossoms like a rose.

102: The angels are telling you to speak your truth, set hearts ablaze. Your authentic voice has the power to ignite souls, challenge perspectives, and inspire change.

103: Faith is your anchor, steady and strong. Let unwavering faith guide you through challenges, reminding you that you're never alone.

104: Embrace change, break free from limitations. Release those holding you back, and soar towards a sky filled with possibilities.

105: Build a refuge of peace, a haven for all. Create spaces where weary souls find solace and connections deepen.

106: Delve deeper into your spirit, uncover hidden knowledge. Seek inner wisdom, explore the depths of your spirit, and let understanding guide you.

107: The universe wants you to acknowledge your worth, a diamond in the rough. Recognize your intrinsic value, the potential waiting to be unearthed. Let your worth shine brightly.

108: Share your gifts, heal and inspire. Use your gifts to uplift others, heal spirits, and inspire them to embrace their own radiance.

109: Closure whispers farewell, lessons learned. Release the past with gratitude for its lessons, preparing the ground for new beginnings.

110: Angels whisper of endless possibilities. Embrace the exciting doors before you, and step into a world where anything is possible.

111: A fresh page awaits! New beginnings dance with amplified intuition, whispering of a spiritual awakening. Manifest your dreams with bold strokes, your inner compass guides you now.

112: The cosmos is telling you to manifest your potential, let your dreams solidify into grand structures. The world awaits your masterpiece, a testament to your spirit and unwavering focus.

113: Let your voice echo through the cosmos! Share your wisdom, express your truth, and light the way for others with your unique words of brilliance.

114: Believe in your ability to learn, evolve, and overcome challenges. Embrace failures as opportunities to grow and refine your approach.

115: Embrace the wind of change, like a leaf on the breeze. Adapt with grace, release the past like autumn leaves, and embrace the new beginnings in love or relationships that whisper on the horizon. The universe dances with possibility.

116: Nurture the garden of your heart, let love bloom within. Cherish your family, create a haven of harmony, and let love be the sun that warms your soul and strengthens your bonds. Together, you bloom amidst life's storms.

117: Discover your inner sanctuary. Listen to your intuition, and let your spiritual journey guide you toward enlightenment. In stillness, you find the key to your true purpose.

118: Abundance rains down upon you, a reward for your unwavering spirit! Believe in your worth, manifest your highest potential, and bask in the material success that reflects your achievements. You deserve prosperity, claim it with gratitude.

119: Release the burdens. Forgive yourself and the past, let go of what weighs you down, and make space for the new beginnings that shimmer on the horizon. Forgiveness is the gateway to abundance, open your heart and receive.

120: The angels encourage you to close one chapter, open the next. The future is a canvas of endless possibilities, paint it with courage and joy.

121: You are on the right path! New beginnings dance in your creative pursuits or career. Follow your passions, trust your inner fire, and paint your masterpiece on the world.

122: Seek balance in all aspects, nurture cooperation, and let your journey lead you to the one who resonates with your deepest melody. Your soul mate awaits, their song harmonizing with yours.

123: Trust your inner compass, let intuition guide your way. Release fears that hold you back, embrace change as the wind beneath your wings. The universe whispers exciting adventures, be ready to soar.

124: Angels walk beside you, whispering support and guidance. Feel their presence, trust their reassuring hand, and know you are never alone on your path. Their wings embrace you in every challenge.

125: Open your heart, beautiful soul! New beginnings blossom in love and relationships. Vulnerability is strength, embrace it, and let love paint your world with vibrant hues.

126: Nestle your spirit in a haven of peace. Nurture your family, cherish home as your sanctuary, and find inner peace in the warmth of your nest. You are safe, loved, and forever held.

127: Honing your spiritual gifts is the journey within. Embrace your intuition, let inner wisdom illuminate your path, and connect with your spirit guides. They whisper guidance in the quiet moments, listen close.

128: Abundance showers upon you, a reward for your unwavering spirit! Believe in your worth, manifest your desires, and bask in the recognition that reflects your achievements. You are worthy, celebrated, and radiant.

129: Be a beacon of hope. Service to others is your calling, use your gifts to heal the world, and mend the cracks with your compassion. Remember, your light illuminates the path for others.

130: Rise with the strength of a mountain, claim your inner power! Take control of your life, and paint your destiny with bold strokes. You are the author of your story, write it with courage and brilliance.

131: A fresh page beckons! Dive into new beginnings, take bold action, and manifest your dreams. The universe awaits your next chapter, written with unwavering spirit.

132: Harmony is the key message from the universe. Seek balance in all aspects, nurture cooperation, and find common ground. Together, you build a symphony of success.

133: Unleash your voice, let your creativity soar! Express yourself authentically, communicate with heart, and share your unique gifts with the world. Your voice inspires and uplifts.

134: Brick by solid brick, build your foundation. Embrace practicality, roll up your sleeves, and lay the groundwork for your ambitious aspirations. Steadiness fuels your ascent.

135: Embrace the winds of change! Adapt with grace, release the past like autumn leaves, and grasp the vibrant new opportunities swirling around you. The future shimmers with possibility.

136: Nurture your loved ones, create a haven of support. Let love be the sun that warms your family, and build a fortress of strength together. In unity, you thrive.

137: Embrace your spirituality, listen to your intuition, and connect with your higher self. In stillness, you find your guiding light.

138: Believe in your financial worth, manifest prosperity, and claim the success your hard work deserves. You are worthy, prosperous, and unstoppable.

139: Angels speak of hope. Use your gifts to make a difference, serve others with compassion, and heal the world with your unique talents. Remember, your light illuminates the path for others.

140: This message from the universe is of the new chapters waiting to unfold. The future is a limitless horizon, step into it with courage and optimism.

141: Hone your intuition, seek enlightenment, and master your connection to your divine purpose. Your inner compass guides you to a life radiating with light and meaning.

142: Manifest your potential, turn dreams into tangible structures, and leave a mark on the world. Your dedication shapes a future that inspires.

143: Let your voice echo through time! Share your wisdom, express your truth, and illuminate the path for others with your unique words.

144: Embrace practicality, organize your thoughts, and find stability in your career. A clear mind and steady steps fuel your ascent.

145: Dance with change, like a willow in the wind. Adapt with grace, release the past, and embrace the new chapters waiting to unfold. The universe whispers exciting adventures.

146: Create a haven of warmth and harmony. Let love be the sun that warms your family, and build a home of strength together. In unity, you bloom amidst life's storms.

147: Seek your inner knowledge. Listen to your intuition, and let your spiritual journey guide you toward inner peace. In stillness, you find the key to your true purpose.

148: Abundance is a reward for your unwavering spirit! Believe in your worth, manifest prosperity, and claim the success your hard work deserves.

149: Angels hold you in their embracel. Forgive yourself and the past, let go of what weighs you down, and make space for the new beginnings that shimmer on the horizon. Forgiveness clears the path to abundance, open your heart and receive.

150: A fresh page awaits, beckoning you to new beginnings! Dive into spiritual growth, manifest your dreams with bold action, and remember your profound connection to the universe. You are limitless, evolving, and divinely connected.

151: Love's blossom unfolds anew! New beginnings dance in your relationships, promising positive growth. Trust your intuition, let your heart guide you, and embrace the joy of connection.

152: Harmony resonates through cooperation, dear soul. Seek balance in all aspects, nurture teamwork, and find compromise. Together, you weave a symphony of success.

153: Unleash your creative spirit, let your talents fly! Express yourself authentically, share your inspiration, and radiate confidence. You are a source of light and joy for others.

154: Before reaching for the stars, ensure you have a solid foundation in place. This could involve building financial stability, developing necessary skills, or cultivating supportive relationships.

155: Angels speak of change! Adapt with grace, release the past like autumn leaves, and grasp the vibrant new experiences swirling around you. The future shimmers with possibility.

156: Nurture family, create a haven of security and love. Let love be the sun that warms your relationships. In unity, you find solace and strength.

157: Seek the quiet whispers within and connect with your higher self. In stillness, you find your guiding light.

158: Financial abundance is coming your way! Trust in your value, manifest your desires, and claim the success your hard work deserves.

159: Use your gifts to make a difference, serve others with compassion, and heal the world with your unique talents. Remember, your light illuminates the path for others.

160: Close one chapter, open the next. Embrace the lessons learned, release what no longer serves you, and prepare for the new beginnings waiting to unfold. The future is a limitless horizon, step into it with courage and optimism.

161: A fresh canvas beckons, artist! Dive into new beginnings in your creativity or career. Take bold action, follow your passions, and paint your masterpiece on the world. Your spirit yearns to create, unleash it!

162: Harmony sings in the rhythm of cooperation. Seek balance in all aspects, nurture partnerships, and find your soul mate in the melody of shared goals and dreams.

163: The universe says to trust yourself. Release doubt and negativity, embrace positive change, and dance with the wind of destiny. The universe whispers exciting adventures.

164: Angels walk beside you, whispering support and guidance. Feel their presence, trust their reassuring hand, and know you are never alone on your path. Their wings embrace you in every challenge, in every moment of connection with loved ones.

165: Open your heart, let love bloom anew! New beginnings blossom in your relationships. Vulnerability is strength, embrace it, heal old wounds with forgiveness, and let love paint your world with vibrant hues.

166: Nestled in the warmth of family, find your safe haven. Nurture your loved ones, cherish home as your sanctuary, and discover inner peace in the comfort of their embrace. You are safe, loved, and forever held.

167: Honing your spiritual gifts is the journey within. Embrace your intuition, let inner wisdom illuminate your path, and connect with your spirit guides. They whisper guidance in the quiet moments, listen close, and unlock your hidden potential.

168: Abundance rains down upon you, a reward for your unwavering spirit! Believe in your worth, manifest prosperity, and savor the success your hard work deserves. You are worthy, celebrated, and radiant, bask in the joy of recognition.

169: Be a lightworker, a beacon of healing. Use your gifts to mend the cracks in the world, share your compassion, and make a difference. Remember, your light illuminates the path for others, your touch brings solace.

170: The future is a limitless horizon, step into it with courage and optimism. Your spiritual growth is a continuous journey, ever-evolving and ever-illuminating.

171: A fresh page beckons! Dive into new beginnings, take bold action, manifest your dreams, and trust in your inner compass. You are the architect of your destiny, build it with unwavering spirit.

172: Harmony is the key. Nurture teamwork, and find common ground. Together, you weave a tapestry of success, stronger threads woven in collaboration.

173: Unleash your unique voice and release your creativity! Express yourself authentically, communicate with heart, and share your unique perspective. Your voice is a gift, use it to inspire and uplift.

174: Brick by brick, lay the groundwork for your aspirations. Embrace practicality, roll up your sleeves, and build a solid foundation. Steady steps and unwavering effort fuel your ascent.

175: Be ready for great change. Embrace it and release the past like autumn leaves, and grasp the vibrant new opportunities swirling around you..

176: Create a haven of support for your loved ones. Let love be the sun that warms your family, and build a strong bond together. Unconditional love is the foundation of your greatest joy.

177: Seek the quiet whispers within, discover your inner sanctuary. Embrace your spirituality, listen to your intuition, and connect with your higher self. In meditation and stillness, you find your guiding light.

178: Abundance showers upon you, a reward for your relentless spirit! Believe in your worth, manifest prosperity, and express gratitude for your blessings. Use your wealth wisely, for it is a tool to uplift and empower others.

179: Be a lightworker, a beacon of hope. Use your talents to make a difference, serve others with compassion, and heal the world with your unique gifts.

180: Release what no longer serves you, and prepare for the new beginnings that shimmer on the horizon. The universe whispers of a spiritual awakening, let it guide you on your journey.

181: Dive into new beginnings, follow your passions with fiery spirit, and paint your dreams onto the world. Your creativity is a beacon, illuminating your path and inspiring others.

182: Seek balance in all aspects, nurture cooperation, and find your soul mate in the melody of shared goals and dreams. Together, your song creates a beautiful symphony.

183: Trust your inner compass, let intuition guide your way. Release fears and embrace new beginnings with childlike excitement, and dance with the wind of destiny.

184: Angels walk beside you, whispering support and guidance. Feel their presence, trust their reassuring hand, and know you are never alone on your path. Their wings embrace you in every challenge, boosting your confidence and belief in yourself.

185: Open your heart, let love bloom anew! New beginnings blossom in your relationships. Vulnerability is strength, embrace it, heal old wounds with forgiveness and love.

186: Nestled in the warmth of home, find your sanctuary. Nurture your loved ones, cherish family as your haven, and discover inner peace in the comfort of simplicity. In the quiet moments, joy blossoms amidst life's storms.

187: Honing your spiritual gifts is the journey within. Embrace your intuition, let inner wisdom illuminate your path, and connect with your angels.

188: Abundance rains down upon you, a reward for your unwavering spirit! Believe in your worth, manifest prosperity, and celebrate your achievements with pride.

189: Use your talents to mend the cracks in the world, share your compassion, and make a difference. Remember, your light illuminates the path for others, your touch brings solace.

190: Close one chapter, open the next. The future is a limitless horizon, step into it with courage and optimism. Your spiritual growth is a continuous journey, ever-evolving and ever-illuminating.

191: A fresh page shimmers, dear one. Take the pen, trust your hand, and write your story anew. The cosmos whispers, "Believe in your dreams, and they shall bloom."

192: Seek balance, weave threads of collaboration, and find strength in the tapestry of shared goals. Remember, many hands build mountains.

193: Let your voice echo, unique and vibrant. Share your colors with the world, paint your truths with bold strokes. Your perspective is a precious gem, let it shine.

194: Ground your dreams in the bedrock of effort. Build a solid foundation, and watch your aspirations rise like towers against the dawn. Hard work is the magic dust of achievement.

195: Release the past, let go of what no longer serves, and step into the vibrant dance of new possibilities. The future whispers secrets in the rustling leaves.

196: The angels are reminding you that home is where the soul finds solace.

197: Your spirit guides urge you to find peace in the quiet moments of meditation.Seek the hush within, where wisdom whispers secrets to your soul.

198: Abundance flows like a river, a reward for your open heart and tireless spirit. Trust your worth, let prosperity bloom, and remember to share the water, for true wealth lies in giving.

199: Your gifts are like starlight, meant to illuminate the world. Use them to mend the cracks, to heal the hurting, and to make a difference.

200: Release what no longer serves, embrace the wisdom you've gained, and prepare for the spiritual awakening that awaits. The universe whispers, "You are ever-evolving, ever-becoming."

201: Leap across the threshold of your comfort zone, take action, and manifest your dreams. The stars whisper, "Dare to soar, and the cosmos will catch you."

202: Collaboration is your key! Seek balance, listen to others, and find common ground. Remember, even stars shine brighter together.

203: Your angels are sending a message to explore your talents. Your creativity is a gift, use it to inspire.

204: Ground your dreams in the soil of hard work. Plant your aspirations, and watch them bloom like celestial gardens. Remember, dedication is the fertilizer for success.

205: Release the past, let go of what no longer serves, and explore new experiences. The next chapter promises to be exciting!.

206: The Universe reminds you to make family a priority., let love be the sun that warms your loved ones. Create a haven of support and unconditional love.

207: Seek the silent spaces within, where whispers of ancient wisdom echo. Connect with your higher self, trust your intuition, and delve into the secrets of the universe through stillness.

208: Abundance flows your way! Trust the rhythm of wealth, manifest your prosperity, and remember that the universe will echo your positive vibrations.

209: Your angels urge you to share your gifts with the world. Don't hide your talents.

210: Every chapter holds its lessons, every ending whispers new beginnings. Release what no longer serves, embrace the wisdom you've gleaned, and prepare for the spiritual odyssey that awaits.

211: A fresh canvas stretches before you! Follow the brushstrokes of your passion, paint your purpose onto the world with vibrant hues.

212: Harmony hums in the melody of partnership, dear one. Seek balance and understanding, and find your soul mate in the rhythm of shared goals.

213: Trust the whispers of your heart, let intuition be your compass. Release fear like a feather on the wind, and embrace new beginnings.

214: Angels walk beside you, their wings brushing away doubt. Feel their support, listen to their guidance, and believe in the strength you hold within. Remember, you are never alone, even in the darkest corners of the sky.

215: Open your heart, let love paint a new dawn in your relationships. Heal old wounds with forgiveness, like moonlight erasing shadows. Vulnerability is strength, embrace it, and watch love bloom like constellations in your soul.

216: Nestled in the warmth of home, find your sanctuary. Nurture your loved ones, let family be the starlight in your haven, and discover inner peace in the quiet moments of togetherness.

217: Hone your celestial gifts, for they are whispers of your inner wisdom. Connect with your spirit guides, seek solace in meditation, and listen to the secrets the universe shares in the stillness.

218: The universe will send a reward for your unwavering spirit. Your manifestations for abundance will pay off with your hard work and aligned actions!

219: Your Angels are lifting you up and applauding your efforts! You are on the right path!

220: Stop worrying about the past. There is such a bright future ahead of you once you leave the past behind.

221: Deepen your spiritual connection through prayer, meditation, or spending time in nature. Ask for guidance and support, and trust that your angels are always with you.

222: Angels whisper of togetherness. Seek balance, weave threads of unity, and find strength in the tapestry of shared goals. Cooperation, both personal and profession, is key

223: Speak your truth and stop hiding your true self. The angels lift you high. Be proud of yourself!

224: Ground your dreams in the bedrock of effort. Brick by steady brick, build a foundation for your aspirations, and watch them rise like towers against the cosmic dawn.

225: Embrace the winds of change, like a comet streaking across the sky. Release the past, let go of what no longer serves, and soar into the vibrant constellations of new possibilities.

226: Create a haven of support for loved ones where roots grow strong and hearts are full with unconditional love.

227: Seek the quiet spaces within, where whispers of celestial wisdom echo. Connect with your higher self, trust your intuition, and delve into the secrets of the universe through stillness. Remember, knowledge hides in the quiet corners of your soul.

228: Abundance flows like a celestial river, drawn to your open heart and boundless spirit. Trust the rhythm of wealth, manifest your prosperity, and remember, sharing its waters makes the tide rise for all.

229: Your gifts are like stardust, meant to mend the cracks in the world. Use them to bring solace, to make a difference, and to heal the hurting. Your compassion is a beacon, guiding others towards a brighter constellation.

230: Every ending is a new beginning, a supernova birthing new stars. Release what no longer serves, embrace the wisdom you've gleaned, and prepare for the spiritual odyssey that awaits.

231: The universe is urging you to follow your dreams!

232: Feel the angels embrace. Seek love within yourself and it will lead to your soulmate.

233: Something new and exciting is on the horizon. The universe hums with the secrets of adventure, listen close.

234: Angels walk beside you, their wings brushing away doubt. Feel their support, listen to their guidance, and trust the strength you hold within.

235: Open your heart, let love paint a new dawn in your relationships. Heal old wounds with forgiveness, like moonlight erasing shadows. Vulnerability is strength, embrace it, and watch love bloom like constellations in your soul.

236: Nestled in the warmth of home, find your sanctuary. Nurture your loved ones, let family be the starlight in your haven, and discover inner peace in the quiet moments of togetherness.

237: Hone your celestial gifts, for they are whispers of your inner wisdom. Connect with your spirit guides, seek solace in meditation, and listen to the secrets the universe shares in the stillness.

238: Abundance showers upon you, a reward for your unwavering spirit. Trust your worth, let prosperity dance like meteors across your sky, and celebrate your achievements with the laughter of the stars.

239: Your talents are meant to mend the cracks in the world. Use them to heal the hurting, to make a difference, and to bring solace with your compassion.

240: Every chapter holds its lessons, every ending whispers new beginnings. Release what no longer serves, embrace the wisdom you've gleaned, and prepare for the spiritual metamorphosis that awaits.

241: Changes are coming. The angels are saying to trust in the journey. Everything will work out.

242: Seek balance and collaboration in your professional life. This will lead to advancement.

243: Share your perspective with confidence and you will be rewarded. Your voice is a precious gem, let it inspire.

244: Your angels are applauding your hard work! Keep building your future with this steady stream of positivity and you will make your dreams a reality.

245: Embrace the winds of change. Release the past, let go of what no longer serves, and dance with new possibilities.

246:Remember to nurture your relationships, both friends and family. Show them the unconditional love you feel and it will be returned back to you.

247:Connect with your higher self through meditation, yoga or simple quiet time. Trust your intuition, and delve into the secrets of the universe through stillness.

248: Wealth flows towards you, manifest your prosperity, and remember to show gratitude for all the abundance in your lifeI.

249: Use your unique talents to repair damage and bring comfort. Make a positive impact and offer solace to those in need. Let your empathy guide others towards a more hopeful reality.

250: The angels are guiding you to tap into your inner wisdom and make decisions based on your gut feeling rather than fear or doubt.

251: Significant transformations are coming, and you're well-equipped to handle them. Be open to new opportunities, accept life's ebbs and flows, and trust that all changes ultimately lead to your highest good.

252: Harmony sings in the rhythm of partnership, dear one. Seek balance, weave threads of understanding, and find your soul mate in the dance of shared goals. Remember, two stars shine brighter in harmonious duality.

253: Before embarking on any new journey, cultivate inner peace and stability. Meditation, spending time in nature, and connecting with loved ones can help.

254: Angels walk beside you, their wings offering unwavering support. Feel their guidance, listen to their reassuring whispers, and believe in the strength you hold within. Remember, their encouragement whispers hope in every step.

255: Your angels are urging you to embrace change as a positive force in your life. It's time to let go of old patterns, beliefs, and habits that no longer serve you and open yourself to new possibilities and experiences.

256: Your angels are assuring you that your material and spiritual needs are being taken care of. Have faith in the divine plan and release any worries or fears about your finances or well-being.

257: Hone your celestial gifts, for they are whispers of your inner wisdom. Connect with your spirit guides, seek solace in meditation, and deepen your connection with the universe through stillness.

258: The Universe is conspiring to bring you abundance in all its forms. This could be financial prosperity, creative fulfillment, or an abundance of love and support. Trust that you deserve abundance and open yourself to receiving it.

259: The angels say to release the past. This could be anything from limiting beliefs and negative habits to unhealthy relationships and outdated material possessions. Release attachment and create space for new beginnings.

260: The spirit guides whisper that positive changes are coming your way. Be open to new opportunities and embrace them with a positive attitude.

261: Fresh start awaits! Take initiative, trust yourself, manifest your dreams. The cosmos says: "Believe in your own power, and it will light your way."

262: Harmony thrives in cooperation. Seek balance, find common ground, work together. Remember: stronger as one, not alone.

263: Share your unique voice, authentically. Express yourself with confidence, your perspective matters. Be true to you, inspire others.

264: Build your dreams on hard work. Brick by brick, create a solid foundation, achieve your goals. Stability is your anchor, groundedness your guide.

265: Step outside your comfort zone and embrace new challenges and opportunities. The angels are supporting you to expand your horizons and discover new dimensions of yourself.

266: Love is your family's haven. Nurture them, create a supportive space, love unconditionally. Unity is your strength, your soul's song.

267: Seek inner wisdom, connect with your higher self. Trust intuition, listen for guidance, have faith. Stillness reveals your path, your inner voice speaks.

268: Open your heart to abundance. Trust the flow of wealth, manifest your prosperity, share wisely. Gratitude paints your path, generosity your guiding light.

269: Use your talents to make a difference. Heal, bring solace, and show compassion. Your humanitarian spirit shines, making the world a brighter place.

270: The angels are encouraging you to find balance in your life, both internally and externally. This includes balancing your work and personal life, maintaining healthy relationships, and taking care of your physical and mental well-being.

271: Listen to your inner voice. Your intuition holds the key to navigating changes and making positive choices. Don't dismiss your gut feelings, and embrace the guidance they offer.

272: Harmony thrives in compromise, dear one. Seek balance, find common ground, and weave a tapestry of shared goals. Remember: collaboration builds bridges, not walls.

273: Your inner voice guides you towards positive pathways. Pay attention to your gut feelings and act with faith and clarity.

274: Your thoughts and intentions have power. Hold onto your dreams with unwavering faith and know that the Universe is conspiring to help you achieve them.

275: Pay close attention to your inner voice, gut feelings, and dreams. Your intuition is guiding you towards the right path and choices. Have faith in your ability to make the best decisions for yourself.

276: Examine your current path and ask yourself if it aligns with your true calling. If not, it's time to make adjustments and pursue what truly resonates with your soul.

277: Amidst external changes, maintain inner stability and a strong foundation. Trust your intuition and make decisions based on your inner wisdom.

278: Your angels are urging you to trust in the divine plan and the unfolding of events. Stay positive, release doubts, and let your intuition guide you towards the right decisions.

279: Fresh opportunities and exciting chapters are unfolding before you. Step out of your comfort zone, be open to new ideas, and allow yourself to explore uncharted territories.

280: This is a reminder that you are on a spiritual journey and your experiences are helping you evolve. Stay open to learning and growing from challenges and setbacks.

281: New canvas beckons, artist! Ignite passions, chase purpose, expand creativity. Bloom boldly, fill the universe with your light.

282: Harmony thrives in partnership. Seek balance, weave understanding, find your soul mate in shared goals. Two stars shine brighter together.

283: Transformation is essential for growth. Be open to new opportunities, let go of outdated patterns, and welcome positive shifts in your life.

284: Angels walk beside you, offering unwavering support. Feel their guidance, believe in your strength. Hope echoes in every step.

285: Embrace your individuality and express your true self without fear of judgment. Embrace your unique talents, gifts, and passions, and share them with the world.

286: Change is often a catalyst for growth. Embrace new opportunities and challenges with a positive attitude, knowing that they are leading you towards a more fulfilling life.

287: Pay attention to your intuition and inner guidance. Your thoughts and desires hold power, so focus on visualizing and manifesting your positive intentions.

288: Angels encourage you to collaborate with others, share your gifts, and build strong partnerships. When you work together, you can achieve greater things than you can on your own.

289: This message urges you to deepen your connection with your higher self and the divine. Engage in spiritual practices like meditation, prayer, or spending time in nature.

290: The angels are prompting you to collaborate with others or join forces towards a common goal. Remember, teamwork can bring greater success than going it alone.

291: Take charge, trust yourself, manifest your dreams. The cosmos says: Believe in your power, it guides your way.

292: Harmony thrives in collaboration. Seek balance, find common ground, work together. Stronger united, not alone.

293: The angels urge you to channel your energy into creative pursuits that bring you joy and express your unique talents. Your creativity can be a powerful tool for manifestation.

294: Don't just visualize and hope. The angels urge you to take focused action steps, driven by your intuition and aligned with your highest purpose. Perseverance and hard work are key to manifesting your desires.

295: Let go of fear, self-doubt, and any limiting beliefs that are holding you back. The angels are encouraging you to believe in yourself, your abilities, and the possibilities that lie ahead.

296: Foster love, compassion, and understanding in your relationships with others. Create a harmonious home environment and prioritize quality time with loved ones.

297: Positive changes are unfolding, leading you towards greater alignment with your purpose. Embrace these changes with an open heart and trust that they are for your highest good.

298: Open your heart to abundance. Trust the flow of wealth, manifest your prosperity, share wisely. Gratitude paints your path, generosity your guiding light.

299: Use your talents to make a difference. Heal, bring solace, and show compassion. Your humanitarian spirit shines, making the world a brighter place.

300: The angels remind of the importance of listening to your inner voice and making choices based on gut feeling rather than external pressures. It's a reminder to connect with your higher self and seek guidance from your wisdom and inner knowing.

301: Invest in your personal development. Learn new skills, expand your knowledge, and nurture your physical and emotional well-being.

302: Harmony thrives in collaboration, dear one. Seek balance, find common ground, weave a tapestry of shared goals. Remember: stronger together, integrated, not divided.

303: Unleash your creative spirit, share your gifts with the world. Express yourself with confidence, find your unique voice, paint your stories with optimism. Your vision inspires, ignite the world!

304: While pursuing your dreams, don't neglect the foundation of your life. Maintain balance in your relationships, finances, and health to create a solid platform for your expansion.

305: Embrace the winds of change, let go of what no longer serves. New opportunities dance on the horizon, welcome them with open arms.

306: Remember to take care of your own physical, emotional, and spiritual needs. Engage in activities that bring you joy and peace, and prioritize your well-being.

307: This is a time for introspection and spiritual growth. Connect with your higher self, seek knowledge, and embark on a journey of self-discovery.

308: Don't just wait for abundance to fall into your lap. Take inspired action, set clear goals, and put your intentions into the Universe. Your thoughts and actions create your reality, so choose them wisely.

309: Use your talents and gifts to make a positive impact on the world. Practice empathy, offer kindness, and contribute to causes close to your heart.

310: Release the past, embrace the lessons learned, and prepare for the boundless expansion that awaits. Spiritual awakening is not a destination, but a journey of ever-evolving light. Ascend into your highest potential.

311: Believe in yourself and your potential. Stay optimistic, cultivate gratitude, and trust that the universe is working in your favor. Your positive energy will attract positive outcomes.

312: Harmony resonates in the duet of partnership. Seek balance, weave threads of understanding, find your soul mate in the dance of shared goals. Remember: two stars shine brighter in harmonious duality, forever connected.

313: See your goals and dreams clearly in your mind's eye. Positive visualization combined with focused action can help you manifest your desires.

314: You don't have to walk this path alone. Work with others who share your vision, seek guidance from mentors, and trust in the support of the Universe.

315: Maintain a positive mindset and focus on the good things in your life. Trust that the changes you're experiencing are leading you towards a more fulfilling and aligned path.

316: Pay attention to your inner guidance and gut feelings. Your intuition is often aligned with your soul's purpose and can provide valuable insights..

317: Connect with your spirit guides, seek solace in meditation, deepen your cosmic connection to the universe.

318: While pursuing abundance, don't neglect your inner peace and well-being. Practice self-care, nurture your relationships, and find joy in the present moment.

319: While embracing change and pursuing personal growth, remember to nurture inner peace and maintain healthy relationships. Find joy in the present moment and navigate challenges with grace.

320: This message signifies a period of transformation and new beginnings. It encourages you to embrace positive changes and adapt to new circumstances with an open mind and a positive attitude.

321: Angels encourage you to strengthen your spiritual connection. Meditation, prayer, and spending time in nature can help you tap into your inner wisdom and receive guidance from your angels.

322: Harmony sings in the dance of collaboration. Find common ground, weave threads of teamwork, and let social harmony bloom.

323: Work together with like-minded individuals who support your goals. Harmony and cooperation can amplify your positive intentions.

324: A positive attitude attracts positive energy and fuels your manifestation journey. Focus on the good, overcome doubt, and keep your faith burning bright.

325: Nurture your connection with your angels and spiritual guides. Ask for their guidance, support, and protection as you navigate change and personal growth.

326: The universe assures you that the changes unfolding in your life are aligned with your highest good, even if they feel challenging.

327: Strive for balance in all areas of your life, including work, relationships, and personal well-being. Maintain inner peace and harmony amidst external fluctuations.

328: Abundance flows towards your open heart and grateful spirit. Share your wealth wisely, expand your abundance consciousness, and illuminate the world with generosity.

329: Even amidst moments of uncertainty, know that the Universe is guiding you toward your highest good. Release fear and anxieties, and trust that all experiences, even challenging ones, are serving your journey.

330: The universe emphasizes the importance of finding balance in your life, both internally and externally. It reminds you to build healthy relationships, seek cooperation, and maintain peace within yourself.

331: Ignite your passions, chase your purpose, expand your creativity and self-expression. The cosmos whispers: Bloom boldly, and your light will paint the universe.

332: The angels are reassuring you that you're on the right path and they are supporting your journey. Trust their guidance and stay optimistic.

333: Be thankful for the blessings in your life and the guidance you receive from your angels. Gratitude attracts more abundance and joy.

334: The Universe has its own perfect timing. Be patient, trust the process, and know that everything is unfolding exactly as it should.

335: Prepare for significant shifts in your personal or professional life. These changes, though seemingly daunting, are divinely guided and will propel you towards a brighter future. Trust the process and embrace the unknown with excitement.

336: Don't resist the transformations taking place. Embrace them with an open heart and mind, knowing they will lead you to a more fulfilling and aligned path.

337: Build strong, supportive relationships based on trust and cooperation. Work together with others to achieve your goals and manifest your collective desires.

338: True abundance involves not just receiving but also giving. Share your blessings with others, express gratitude, and cultivate a giving spirit.

339: Your angels cheer you on! Your intuition is guiding you in the right direction. Pay attention to your gut feelings, dreams, and inner nudges. They will lead you towards the path of personal growth and fulfillment.

340: Every chapter holds lessons, every ending whispers new beginnings. Release what no longer serves, embrace the wisdom, prepare for the spiritual odyssey. Growth is a cosmic dance, ever-expanding, ever-ascending.

341: The angels are reminding you to trust in the divine plan and have faith in your abilities. They are with you on your journey and will guide you through any challenges.

342: The angels are encouraging you to forgive, move on, and embrace new possibilities.

343: Before embarking on any journey, find stillness within yourself. Let go of anxieties and doubts, and connect with your inner wisdom. This will guide your actions and attract positive experiences.

344: This message reminds you of your inherent strength and potential. Believe in your abilities, trust your intuition, and step forward with confidence.

345: This is a time to step into your power and unleash your unique talents and gifts. Don't be afraid to express yourself authentically and pursue your passions with unwavering confidence. Remember, you were born to shine!

346: This message encourages you to pursue what truly sets your soul on fire, and trust that the Universe will support your endeavors.

347: Your inner voice is your greatest guide. Pay close attention to your gut feelings, dreams, and intuitive nudges, as they hold valuable insights for your journey.

348: Abundance flows to your grateful heart and open spirit. Share wisely, expand your consciousness, illuminate the world.

349: Talents heal the world, use yours with compassion. Make a difference, empathy is your light, illuminate the path for others.

350: Angels encourage you to explore your spirituality, embrace your values, and connect with the divine.

351: A period of growth and transformation is coming. Be open to new experiences, let go of what no longer serves you, and embrace the positive changes that are coming your way.

352: This is a sign from your angels to embrace your creative talents and use them to bring light and positivity into your life.

353: The universe is reminding you that transformation is inevitable, and it often begins from within. Be open to new ideas, perspectives, and experiences. Let go of limiting beliefs and step into your full potential.

354: Angels walk beside you, their wings offering unwavering support. Feel their guidance, believe in your strength, know you are divinely connected.

355: The universe nudges you to connect with your inner wisdom and discover your true purpose in life. Listen to your intuition, explore new pathways, and don't be afraid to break free from limiting beliefs that hold you back.

356: Find your sanctuary in the warmth of home and community. Nurture loved ones, let joy blossom in simplicity. Inner peace whispers in the quiet moments of togetherness, creating a safe haven for all.

357: The angels say that you're on the right path and making positive progress in your life. It encourages you to stay focused and motivated, trusting that your efforts will bear fruit.

358: Your positive thoughts and actions are attracting abundance into your life. Be open to receiving blessings in various forms, not just material possessions.

359: Change is inevitable and often leads to greater opportunities. Be open to new experiences, release what no longer serves you, and trust that the changes are for your highest good.

360: This is a sign that your positive thoughts and intentions are manifesting into reality. Stay focused on your goals and maintain a positive attitude to attract abundance and success.

361: Your inner voice holds wisdom and guidance. Pay attention to your intuition and trust its direction.

362: Be open to new opportunities and exciting developments in your life. Trust that these changes are divinely guided and will lead you to greater fulfillment

363: Your thoughts and intentions have power. Focus on positivity, visualize your goals, and take inspired action. The Universe is conspiring to support you in achieving your desires.

364: Change is inevitable, but it's also an opportunity for growth. Embrace new opportunities, learn from challenges, and let go of past limitations.

365: Embrace change, let go of past's hold. New opportunities dance, welcome them with open arms, transform and evolve.

366: Invest time and energy in fostering strong connections with loved ones, offering support, and resolving any conflicts with a spirit of forgiveness.

367: The universe encourages you to take inspired action towards your goals and desires. Believe in your ability to manifest your dreams and take consistent steps towards achieving them

368: Focus on your goals and desires with unwavering belief. Take inspired action, stay consistent, and trust that the Universe is conspiring to bring your dreams to fruition.

369: Invest in yourself and your development. Learn new skills, explore your passions, and challenge yourself to expand your horizons. Personal growth leads to greater self-awareness and a more fulfilling life.

370: Angels urge you to release any negativity or burdens from the past that might be holding you back. Forgive yourself and others, and move forward with a clean slate.

371:Take charge, manifest dreams and trust your inner fire. Self-reliance guides your path, independence your wings.

372: Harmony sings in the dance of collaboration. Find common ground, weave threads of understanding, let social harmony bloom. Integration strengthens all, compromise paints a vibrant tapestry.

373: Use your talents and gifts to make a positive impact. Share your ideas, engage in activities that bring you joy, and let your inner light shine through.

374: Before embarking on new ventures, ensure you have a solid foundation. Set realistic goals, work diligently, and create a structure that supports your growth.

375: Let go of anything that no longer serves you, be it past relationships, negative emotions, or limiting habits. Forgive yourself and others, and make space for new experiences and opportunities to flourish.

376: Cultivate a supportive and nurturing environment where you and your loved ones can thrive.

377: This divine message means you're on the verge of discovering your true purpose. Seek opportunities for self-discovery and connect with your inner wisdom to find your unique path.

378: Sometimes, things may not unfold as quickly as you expect. Trust that the Universe has a perfect plan for you and surrender to the flow of life with patience and faith.

379: Discover and pursue your life's purpose. Reflect on your values, talents, and aspirations. How can you use them to serve others and make a positive impact on the world?

380: Take inspired action towards your goals. Trust your instincts, but don't be afraid to take the leap and make your dreams a reality.

381: Ignite your dreams, chase your purpose, expand your creative spirit. Self-expression and confidence are your wings, paint your masterpiece on the universe's canvas.

382: Harmony sings in the duet of partnership, dear one. Seek balance, weave threads of understanding, find your soul mate in the shared rhythm of goals. Remember: in compromise and connection, two flames burn brighter. Relationships blossom in the garden of duality.

383: Embrace new beginnings with an open mind, aligned with the whispers of the universe. Faith guides your steps, excitement fuels your journey.

384: Stay the path. Angelic presence whispers reassurance, encouragement flows with every breath.

385: Remember, even during challenging times, the Universe has your back. Stay positive, trust the divine flow, and know that good things are coming your way. Focus on gratitude and appreciate the blessings that already exist in your life.

386: Your angels are closely supporting you through this period of change. Trust their guidance and have faith that everything is unfolding for your highest good.

387: Expressing gratitude for what you have attracts more abundance into your life. Practice gratitude for the blessings you already have, and trust that the Universe is providing for you.

388: Trust your worth, let prosperity dance, celebrate with gratitude. Remember: true wealth lies in receiving with grace and sharing with generosity.

389: Share your blessings with others, offer support, and act with kindness in your interactions. Your compassionate actions will bring positive energy back to you and contribute to a more harmonious world.

390: Your intuition is guiding you in the right direction, so pay attention to your inner voice and don't be afraid to take risks!

391: Your inner voice holds wisdom and guidance. Pay attention to your intuition and trust its direction.

392: Harmony sings in the dance of collaboration. Find common ground, weave threads of teamwork, and let social harmony blossom. Remember, compromise strengthens the whole, and integration creates a vibrant tapestry of connection.

393: Connect with like-minded individuals who share your vision. Work together towards a common goal, and leverage each other's strengths to achieve greater success.

394: Your thoughts and actions have power. Focus on your dreams, visualize your goals, and take consistent action to make them a reality.

395: Big changes are coming your way, but they're meant to propel you forward. Trust that these changes are for your highest good and embrace them with an open heart..

396: Positive changes are coming your way, leading you towards greater alignment with your true purpose. Embrace these changes with an open heart and mind.

397: Focus on building a stable foundation in your life, both materially and emotionally. This could involve setting clear goals, creating healthy routines, and nurturing supportive relationships.

398: While striving for abundance, don't neglect the importance of balance. Maintain healthy relationships, nurture your well-being, and find joy in the present moment.

399: Even amidst change and growth, strive for inner peace and stability. Practice mindfulness, meditation, or other grounding techniques to maintain balance and navigate challenges with grace.

400: Change is inevitable, and it's an opportunity for growth. Be open to new experiences and don't resist the flow of life.

401: Angels beckon you to take action, step into your personal power and manifest your dreams with boldness. Expansion thrives where leadership dances.

402: Harmony finds its rhythm in collaboration. Seek common ground and build teamwork, let practicality and diplomacy build stability.

403: Your inner voice knows the best path for you. Pay attention to your gut feelings, dreams, and synchronicities. They are guiding you towards your highest good.

404: While individual strength is important, remember the power of collaboration. Work with others, share your knowledge, and build strong partnerships.

405: Embrace the wind of change, let go of the past's grip. New opportunities dance, welcome them with open arms, transform and evolve.

406: Strive for balance in all areas of your life, including relationships, work, and spiritual pursuits. Maintain inner peace and harmony amidst transitions.

407: The angels encourage you to invest in your personal development. Seek knowledge, explore new interests, and challenge yourself to learn and grow in all aspects of your life.

408: You are capable of achieving great things. Believe in your abilities, take calculated risks, and step into your full potential.

409: Your inner voice is your guiding light. Pay attention to your gut feelings, dreams, and intuitive nudges. They will lead you towards the right path and choices.

410: It's time to invest in yourself and your development. Learn new things, expand your horizons, and take care of your physical and mental well-being.

411: Don't wait for things to happen. The angels are encouraging you to take initiative, step outside your comfort zone, and pursue your goals with confidence.

412: The angels stress the importance of finding your inner strength and unwavering faith in yourself. It encourages you to overcome challenges with resilience and determination.

413: Release fears like butterflies, embrace new beginnings with open arms and an aligned heart. Excitement fuels your journey, intuition your guiding light.

414: Don't get lost in the pursuit of your goals. Maintain a healthy balance between work and rest, nurture your relationships, and prioritize your well-being.

415: Your gut feeling is your guide through this transformative period. Pay close attention to your intuition and make decisions based on what feels right, not just what others think.

416: Find solace in the warm embrace of home and family. Cultivate love, compassion, and understanding in your relationships with others and yourself. Offer support and kindness to those around you.

417: Your thoughts and intentions have power. Align your actions with your deepest desires and trust in your ability to manifest your goals.

418: Be thankful for the blessings you already have, and express gratitude for the abundance flowing into your life. This amplifies the positive energy and attracts even more blessings.

419: Don't resist the flow of life, but instead, embrace new beginnings with an open heart and a willingness to learn.

420: The angels are reassuring you that positive changes are on the horizon. Stay optimistic and trust that things are working out for the best.

421: A fresh start beckons, ignite the embers of your dreams with bold action and trust in your independent spirit. Forge your own path, a beacon of inspiration to all.

422: Build a strong foundation in your life, focusing on your priorities and setting clear goals. It's about creating a sense of security and stability in all aspects of your life.

423: Before embarking on any new journey, take time to find inner peace and align your actions with your true purpose.

Seek self-reflection, meditation, or spend time in nature to connect with your intuition.

424: Your angels are saying You have the power and potential to achieve great things! Step into your confidence, trust your abilities, and don't be afraid to take risks..

425: Growth often lies beyond your comfort zone. Don't be afraid to take risks, explore new possibilities, and challenge yourself to evolve.

426: Align your actions with your true values and soul mission. Find meaningful ways to express your talents and gifts in service to others.

427: Angels are expressing their encouragement! Pay attention to your inner wisdom and gut feelings. They will guide you towards the right decisions and opportunities for growth.

428: Your positive thoughts and actions are attracting abundance into your life. Stay focused on your goals, trust the process, and open yourself to receiving blessings in various forms.

429: Seek knowledge, explore new interests, and challenge yourself to step outside your comfort zone. Growth leads to greater fulfillment and purpose.

430: The Universe encourages you to connect with your spiritual side and seek guidance from your angels. Meditation and prayer can be helpful practices.

431: A new chapter dawns, ablaze with creative fire. Let passion ignite your spirit, purpose guide your actions, and expression bloom like a vibrant garden. Your artistry weaves a unique tapestry on the world's stage.

432: This message encourages you to tap into your inner power, face challenges with courage, and trust your ability to overcome obstacles.

433: Angels whisper of transformation. Change is inevitable, but it doesn't have to be disruptive. Embrace positive changes with an open heart and trust that they are leading you towards a better future.

434: Unseen wings of support lift you. Angels walk beside you, their voices urging you to believe. Feel their unwavering encouragement, a chorus of divine connection serenading your path.

435: While navigating personal change, don't neglect the power of support. Surround yourself with positive, encouraging people who believe in you and your journey.

436: This is a reminder to let go of fears and worries that may be holding you back. Trust that you are divinely guided and supported through any challenges.

437: Even amidst change and growth, strive for balance in your life. Take care of your physical and mental well-being, and dedicate time to relaxation and self-care.

438: Your gut feeling is your best guide. Pay attention to its whispers and take inspired action towards your dreams.

Remember, the Universe rewards action aligned with your true purpose.

439: Your angels want you to connect with your soul's calling. Use your talents and gifts to serve others and make a positive impact on the world.

440: The angels remind you that success doesn't come overnight. It requires consistent effort, perseverance, and a commitment to quality work. Be prepared to roll up your sleeves, put in the hours, and stay focused on your vision.

441: The angels urge you to take care of your physical, mental, and emotional well-being. This will allow you to embrace change with greater strength and resilience.

442: The universe wants you to be open to new beginnings, embrace new opportunities, and step into your leadership potential.

443: This is a reminder that while embracing change, don't lose sight of your core values and foundation. Maintain a sense of stability and balance in your life to navigate challenges with grace.

444: New doors are opening for you. Be open to new experiences, explore different paths, and don't be afraid to step outside your comfort zone.

445: Even amidst change, strive for inner peace and stability. Practice mindfulness, meditation, or other grounding techniques to stay centered and aligned with your true purpose..

446: The message speaks of the importance of building a solid foundation in your life, both internally and externally. Focus on self-care, cultivate inner strength, and prioritize tasks that create stability and security.

447: The angels embrace you. Know that you are divinely supported on your journey. Trust in the timing and unfolding of events, even if they seem challenging at times.

448: Your spirit guides encourage you to step outside your comfort zone and embrace new opportunities. These changes, though they may seem daunting, are leading you towards greater fulfillment.

449: Even amidst change, strive for inner balance. Practice mindfulness, meditation, and activities that bring you joy and peace. A calm mind makes better decisions and attracts positive experiences.

450: Building a strong foundation takes time and patience. Don't get discouraged by setbacks or slow progress. Trust that your hard work is creating a solid platform for future achievements.

451: Ignite your artistic spirit, pursue your purpose, and expand your expression with audacious confidence. Your creativity blooms onto the world's stage.

452: The universe encourages you to lay solid groundwork, work diligently, and persevere through challenges.

453: The angels want you to express your unique talents and gifts. Don't be afraid to share your creativity with the world and explore new avenues of self-expression.

454: While embracing new possibilities, ensure you have a strong foundation to support your growth. Work hard, set goals, and take practical steps to achieve them.

455: The angels urge you to be open to new opportunities, embrace change with a positive attitude, and trust that these changes will lead you to a better future.

456: The universe encourages you to embrace teamwork and seek support from others. By working together and utilizing everyone's strengths, you can achieve greater progress and overcome challenges more effectively.

457: Take charge of your thoughts and actions, as they shape your reality. Stay positive, focused, and aligned with your true desires to manifest the life you dream of.

458: While pursuing your goals, remember the importance of teamwork. Collaborate with others who share your vision and build supportive partnerships for mutual success.

459: Be grateful for the blessings in your life, big and small. Share your abundance with others and contribute to building a more compassionate and supportive world.

460: Create systems and routines that support your goals. Set clear objectives, plan your actions, and manage your time effectively. Structure provides stability and helps you stay on track.

461: Tap into your inner power and resilience. Trust your intuition, believe in yourself, and face challenges with courage and determination.

462: This message urges you to embrace change with an open mind, let go of the past, and step outside your comfort zone.

463: Share your unique spark, let confidence ignite. Grounded creativity blooms, your voice a radiant light. Express with boldness, the world awaits your story.

464: Diligence paves your path, a solid foundation built with focus. Goals become reality, discipline your guide. Remember, groundedness fuels your ascent.

465: Embrace the flow, let go of yesterday's hold. New opportunities bloom, adaptability your shield. Transformation awaits, dance with the ever-changing tide.

466: The angels nudge you to strengthen your bonds with loved ones and contribute to your community. Offer support and assistance where needed, and cultivate a sense of belonging

467: Seek the whispers within, your inner compass true. Grounded spirituality lights the way, guiding you through darkness and doubt. Remember, intuition is your celestial map.

468: Claim your power and manifest your dreams. Take charge, bold and fearless, let your spirit lead. Remember, the universe awaits your action.

469: Intuition whispers, practicality guides. Blend wisdom with action, let your spirit unfurl. Remember, grounded spirituality is your compass and fuel.

470: Closure whispers new beginnings, lessons learned pave the way. Release the past, embrace the dawn, a fresh chapter unfolds. Remember, endings are doorways to endless possibilities.

471: The angels are reminding you of your power to create your own reality. Focus on your positive thoughts and intentions, and believe in your ability to manifest your dreams.

472: The universe encourages you to find inner peace, maintain healthy relationships, and trust in the divine plan.

473: Open and honest communication is key to navigating change and building strong relationships. Speak your truth, listen actively, and strive for understanding.

474: Don't neglect your relationships or inner peace while pursuing new opportunities. Find balance between your personal and professional life, and cultivate healthy relationships.

475: The angels nudge you to take action and step into your power. Don't let fear or doubts hold you back from pursuing your dreams.

476: This message signifies positive developments in your financial situation, achieved through hard work, responsibility, and collaboration.

477: Significant shifts and transformations are approaching. Trust that these changes are leading you towards greater alignment with your purpose and embrace them with an open mind.

478: Don't let the pursuit of abundance consume you. Find balance between your material goals and your spiritual well-being. Prioritize self-care, mindfulness, and activities that bring you joy.

479: Your gifts are celestial embers, meant to set the world ablaze with healing and compassion. Use them with unwavering dedication, leaving a trail of light with every touch.

480: While focusing on practicality, remember the importance of spiritual growth. Connect with your higher purpose, practice mindfulness and meditation, and stay centered in your values. A strong spiritual foundation leads to inner peace and resilience.

481: Your intuition is leading you in the right direction. Pay attention to your inner voice, gut feelings, and dreams, and don't be afraid to take action based on them.

482: Find balance between your work life, personal life, and spiritual growth. Avoid neglecting any aspect of your life in pursuit of another. Focus on creating a harmonious flow between your commitments and aspirations.

483: Sometimes, things may not happen as quickly as you'd like. Trust that the Universe has a perfect timing for everything and surrender to the flow of life.

484: Remember to believe in your strength, for you walk hand in hand with the divine, forever guided and loved.

485: Heal old wounds with forgiveness and self-acceptance. Vulnerability strengthens your roots, fostering deeper connections where new beginnings bloom in the fertile ground of open hearts.

486: The universe reminds you to trust the divine plan and have faith that the universe is guiding you towards a better future.

487: Pay close attention to your intuition and gut feelings. They will guide you towards the right choices and opportunities during this period of change.

488: As you receive abundance in your life, remember to express gratitude to the Universe and those who have supported you. Generously share your blessings with others to create a ripple effect of positivity.

489: Humanitarian spirit sings in your heart, empathy your eternal melody. Remember, service to others illuminates the path for all.

490: Remember the importance of building a strong foundation in all areas of your life. This could involve establishing healthy routines, managing your finances responsibly, and developing strong relationships.

491: A new chapter is unfolding in your life. Be open to new opportunities, break free from limiting beliefs, and step into your full potential..

492: Positive changes are coming your way, and they may initially feel unsettling. However, trust that these changes are leading you towards your true purpose and greater fulfillment. Embrace them with an open heart and a willingness to learn.

493: Trust the whispers within, your compass true and ever-present. Let go of fear like autumn leaves, embracing new beginnings with open arms and an aligned mind. Excitement fuels your journey, faith your guiding star.

494: Every experience, even challenging ones, holds valuable lessons. Embrace them as opportunities for growth and learning, and use them to refine your skills and approach.

495: Pay attention to your gut feelings and inner whispers. The universe reminds you that your intuition is a powerful guide, especially during times of change and new opportunities.

496: Your angels are telling you that you are on the right path and have the strength to overcome any challenges. They are encouraging you to stay positive and focused on your goals.

497: While embracing change, strive for inner peace and stability. Maintain healthy relationships, dedicate time to self-care, and find grounding practices to stay balanced amidst the transition.

498: This is a powerful message of positive change and exciting new beginnings. Embrace these changes with an open heart and trust that they are leading you towards a brighter future.

499: The universe encourages you to let go of any negativity, anxieties, or past experiences holding you back. It's a time for closure, forgiveness, and stepping into a new chapter with a fresh perspective.

500: Your hard work and dedication are paying off! The angels assure you that your efforts are leading you towards success. Stay focused on your goals, take consistent action, and trust in the divine timing of your achievements.

501: Don't wait for things to happen to you. Take initiative, set goals, and actively work towards your dreams. Your angels are supporting your every step.

502: Before embarking on new ventures, ensure you have a solid foundation in place. This could involve setting realistic goals, developing necessary skills, and establishing a supportive network. A strong foundation provides stability and confidence as you navigate change.

503: Unleash your unique song, let your voice rise like the morning sun. Share your perspective with unwavering authenticity, painting your story with strokes of optimism and joy. Ignite the embers of inspiration in others, creativity your flame, self-expression your fuel.

504: Sometimes, things may not unfold exactly as you expect. Trust that the Universe has a perfect plan for you and surrender to the flow of life with faith and optimism.

505: Positive changes are on the horizon. This could involve career advancement, exciting new relationships, or personal breakthroughs. Be open to these changes and trust that they will lead you to a more fulfilling life.

506: Your angels urge you to take action and move forward. It's time to put your plans into motion and actively pursue your dreams. However, remember to do so with a solid foundation and careful planning.

507: Open and honest communication is key to navigating change and building strong relationships. Speak your truth with confidence and listen actively to understand others

508: This period is filled with opportunities for personal growth and expansion. Be open to new experiences, embrace learning from all situations, and challenge yourself to step outside your comfort zone.

509: This message signifies a period of significant self-discovery and spiritual growth. Embrace new learning opportunities, explore different paths, and connect with your higher purpose.

510: Don't be afraid to ask for help and guidance. Your angels are always with you, offering support and encouragement. Trust that you have the resources and assistance you need to achieve your dreams.

511: Trust that the Universe has your best interests at heart. Stay optimistic, focus on the good things, and know that even challenges are opportunities for growth.

512: Don't try to go it alone. Reach out to friends, family, or mentors for guidance and support. Collaboration and teamwork can lead to greater success and make the journey more fulfilling.

513: Unleash your creative fire, let your voice rise like a vibrant song. Share your unique perspective with unwavering authenticity, painting your story with strokes of optimism and joy. Embrace new artistic pursuits, your spirit a canvas for inspiration to bloom.

514: Brick by mindful brick, build your dreams on a foundation of unwavering practicality. Diligence guides your steps, resourcefulness your weapon, and goals blossom into reality under the focused light of your spirit.

515: Step outside your comfort zone and embrace new experiences. Don't be afraid to take risks, explore new paths, and seek out adventures that ignite your spirit.

516: Don't neglect your emotional needs and relationships in your pursuit of goals. Find balance and maintain harmony in all aspects of your life. Practice self-care, nurture your loved ones, and contribute to your community.

517: Sometimes, things may not unfold exactly as you expect. Trust that the Universe has a perfect plan for you and surrender to the flow of life with faith and optimism.

518: Abundance flows toward your open heart and grateful spirit. Celebrate prosperity with grace, share your bounty wisely, and remember that true wealth lies in the act of giving and receiving.

519: Don't wait for the perfect moment; take inspired action based on your intuition and aligned with your true calling. The Universe is supporting your endeavors.

520: While striving for success, don't neglect other aspects of your life. Maintain a healthy balance between work and leisure, prioritize your physical and mental well-being, and nurture your relationships.

521: Prioritize your physical and mental well-being. Engage in activities that bring you joy, eat nutritious foods, and get enough sleep. A healthy you is better equipped to handle life's changes.

522: Even amidst change and challenges, strive for inner peace. Practice mindfulness, meditation, or activities that bring you joy and calmness. A peaceful mind makes better decisions and attracts positive experiences.

523: Let go like autumn leaves, fears surrendering to the wind. Embrace new beginnings with a hummingbird's joy, open mind your window to possibilities. Faith unfurls its wings, aligning you with your inner compass.

524: Feather-light whispers brush your cheek, angelic chorus urging you to believe. Feel their unwavering support, a warm embrace reminding you of your divine connection. Accept their celestial hand, guided every step of the way.

525: Angels speak of your inherent talents and abilities. They urge you to believe in yourself, tap into your potential, and share your gifts with the world.

526: This is a message to focus on your family and home life. It might be time to spend more quality time with loved ones, create a nurturing environment, or address any unresolved issues within your family.

527: The angels remind you that your thoughts and intentions have power to shape your reality. Focus on positive affirmations, visualize your desires, and take aligned action to manifest your dreams.

528: Use your talents and gifts to serve others and make a positive impact on the world. Contributing to something bigger than yourself will bring you deep fulfillment and connect you to your soul's purpose.

529: While pursuing personal growth and goals, remember to prioritize inner peace and well-being. Practice self-care, mindfulness, and activities that bring you joy and balance.

530: Success rarely happens overnight. Be patient, persistent, and maintain a positive attitude. Trust that your efforts will eventually lead you to the desired outcome.

531: Embrace new beginnings, trusting your inner compass to navigate uncharted territories. Step into your power, fueled by self-reliance and purpose. Manifest your dreams with unwavering initiative.

532: Seek harmony through cooperation and compromise. Find common ground where teamwork flourishes, building partnerships rooted in mutual respect and social harmony.

533: Unleash your creative spirit, sharing your unique perspective with authenticity and joy. Embrace your passions, igniting inspiration in yourself and others.

534: Lay a sturdy foundation for your goals with practicality and diligence. Focus on tangible results, building step by step with resourcefulness and stability.

535: Embrace change with adaptability and grace. Let go of the past, opening yourself to new opportunities and personal growth. Navigate transitions with an open heart and a willingness to transform.

536: Keep going, your hard work and dedication will soon be rewarded with financial stability and prosperity.

537: Seek wisdom within, deepening your spiritual understanding. Connect with your higher self, guided by faith and intuition, and embrace the journey of self-discovery.

538: Open your heart to abundance, welcoming prosperity with gratitude and generosity. Share your blessings wisely, recognizing the interconnected dance of giving and receiving.

539: Use your talents to serve others, guided by compassion and empathy. Find your purpose in healing and humanitarian work, making a positive impact on the world.

540: Embrace closure as a gateway to new beginnings. Release what no longer serves you, learning from lessons and preparing for fresh perspectives. Embrace the cycles of change, trusting in the unfolding path towards enlightenment.

541: Unleash your creative fire. Follow your passions, not maps. Express your unique spark, and watch your world expand.

542: Seek harmony, not compromise. Find your soulmate in teamwork and respect. Dance the duality of connection, and build a fulfilling partnership.

543: Trust your inner whisper, not fleeting fears. Embrace new beginnings with open arms and faith. Leap into alignment, guided by your intuition's light.

544: Angels whisper encouragement, not empty words. Feel their support, believe in your divine connection, and walk with confidence.

545: Open your heart, let go of past hurts. Forgive, accept, and embrace vulnerability. Love's new beginnings await your courageous step.

546: Build a haven of peace, not just bricks and mortar. Find joy in simple moments, nurture loved ones, and create a community of belonging.

547: Seek mastery, not fleeting trends. Expand your consciousness, listen to inner wisdom, and align with your divine purpose.

548: Embrace abundance, not just material wealth. Recognize your worth, share your blessings, and let gratitude flow like a river.

549: Serve with compassion, not obligation. Use your gifts to heal, inspire, and lightwork the path for others.

550: Release the past, lessons learned in hand. Prepare for new chapters, eyes on enlightenment. Fresh perspectives bloom where endings whisper new beginnings.

551: Trust your gut, take that leap, and manifest your dreams with fiery self-reliance. Remember, the universe applauds your every bold step.

552: Angels assure you that you are divinely supported. Have faith in the timing and unfolding of events, even if they seem confusing at times. Remember, the Universe has your best interests at heart.

553: Unleash your creative spirit, a kaleidoscope blessed by angels. Share your unique spark with authenticity, let joy be your brushstroke, and inspire the world with celestial vibrancy.

554: Build a foundation of dreams, guided by unseen hands. Lay each brick with diligence, resourcefulness your mortar, and watch your goals rise under the sun of universal support. Remember, stability is your crown, tangible results your celestial reward.

555: Embrace the winds of change, whispered by angels unseen. Trust the process, for major transformations pave the way for magnificent manifestations. Let go, ride the cosmic currents, and witness your world blossom anew.

556: While action is encouraged, remember to listen to your inner voice. Remember to trust your intuition and make decisions based on what feels right for you.

557: Dive deep within, seeking the wisdom whispered by angels. Explore your intuition, connect with your higher self, and unlock your spiritual gifts. Remember, guidance flows like a celestial river, use it to illuminate your path and touch the lives of others.

558: Abundance blooms where you open your heart to receive. Release limiting beliefs, let go of scarcity, and embrace prosperity in all aspects of your life. Share your blessings, for the universe thrives on the dance of giving and receiving.

559: Use your talents to make a difference, volunteer your time, and choose a service career fueled by kindness. Remember, you are a vessel of celestial light, illuminating the world around you.

560: Close chapters with gratitude, for lessons learned pave the way for new beginnings. Release the past, let go of what no longer serves, and open your heart to limitless possibilities.

561: A fresh start beckons, fueled by self-trust and independence. Take that bold step, the universe applauds your initiative and inner strength.

562: Find balance and harmony within yourself and in your surroundings. This could involve balancing work and personal life, maintaining inner peace, and fostering healthy relationships.

563: Let your soul sing! Share your unique perspective with the world, a vibrant tapestry woven with optimism and inspiration. Embrace your artistic pursuits, for you are a cosmic brush painting masterpieces on the canvas of existence.

564: Build your dreams on stardust pillars. Lay each brick with practicality, resourcefulness your mortar, and watch your goals climb towards the sun of stability. Remember, tangible results are your celestial reward.

565: While embracing change and excitement, remember the importance of hard work and dedication. The message is to combine your adventurous spirit with your practical side for optimal results.

566: You have the support and guidance of your angels, loved ones, and the universe. It's a reminder to trust in the process and stay grounded even when facing challenges.

567: Expand your consciousness, listen to the whispers of your inner sage, and deepen your spiritual connection.

568: Pay attention to your intuition and inner wisdom. They will guide you towards the right decisions and actions during this transformative period.

569: Use your newly acquired knowledge and wisdom to uplift and guide others. Share your blessings and contribute to a more harmonious world.

570: As you progress on your journey, remember to express gratitude for the blessings you receive. Celebrate your milestones, big and small, to stay motivated and continue moving forward.

571: Don't wait for the right moment or perfect circumstances. Take initiative, make decisions, and move forward with your plans. The Universe supports your action when it aligns with your true purpose.

572: Be open to personal growth and learning new things. Explore new interests, challenge yourself, and invest in your development. This will help you expand your horizons and create a fulfilling life.

573: Trust your inner compass. Let go of fear's grip, embrace new horizons with open arms. Faith lights your path.

574: Angels whisper encouragement. Believe in your divine spark, feel their unwavering support. You are never alone.

575: Focus on your desires and visualize your goals with clarity and positive energy. Trust that your positive thoughts and actions can attract the changes you seek.

576: Build a haven of belonging. Nurture family, find peace in simplicity. Community roots your joy.

577: Changes are coming your way. These changes, though challenging at times, are leading you towards a more fulfilling and aligned path. Embrace them with an open heart and trust that they are for your highest good.

578: The universe showers blessings. Recognize your worth, embrace abundance with an open heart. Share your wealth, let it flow.

579: Trust the divine timing. Sometimes, things may not unfold as quickly as you'd like. Trust that the Universe has a perfect plan for you and surrender to the flow of life with faith and optimism.

580: Close chapters with gratitude. New beginnings whisper from the ashes. Let go, embrace the fresh perspectives that await.

581: Your thoughts and intentions have power. Focus on your goals, visualize your desired outcomes, and take concrete steps to make them a reality. Angels remind you that you are a powerful creator.

582: Don't just dream your desires, take action to make them a reality. Combine your intuition and creativity with practical planning and hard work to manifest your goals.

583: Let your words be like sunbeams, illuminating truth and optimism. Share your unique perspective with the world, for your joy is a beacon that inspires others.

584: Angels encourage you to nurture your dreams and aspirations with care and attention. Develop a clear plan, gather resources, and take consistent action to bring your goals to fruition.

585: Embrace the winds of change, be open to new beginnings, embrace new opportunities, and trust that these changes are leading you towards a better future.

586: You are on the cusp of a positive transformation. This could involve changes in your career, relationships, or personal growth. The message is to embrace these changes with a positive attitude and trust that they will lead you to a better future.

587: While navigating change, keep your inner world grounded and peaceful. Practice mindfulness, meditation, or activities that bring you joy to maintain inner harmony and navigate challenges with grace.

588: Focus your thoughts and actions on your goals, and trust in the Universe to support you in bringing them to fruition.

589: Release any negativity, attachments, or outdated beliefs that are holding you back. It's time to embrace new beginnings and move forward with a lighter heart.

590: Focus on building a stable foundation in all aspects of your life, including your career, relationships, finances, and health. Set clear goals, create a plan, and take consistent action to achieve them.

591: While pursuing your dreams, ensure you have a solid foundation in place. Be organized, manage your time effectively, and take care of your physical and mental well-being.

592: Angels whisper of faith. Things may not unfold exactly as you expect. Trust that the Universe has a plan for you and that any challenges are opportunities for growth.

593: Intuition whispers secrets, not alarms. Let go of fear's icy grip, embrace new beginnings with an open mind and unwavering faith. Alignment awaits, trust your inner compass.

594: Angels dance beside you, not above. Feel their guidance in gentle nudges, reassurance in comforting whispers. Believe in yourself, for you are loved by the cosmic choir.

595: Paint your love with vibrant strokes. Collaborate with a kindred spirit, express your unique perspectives, and ignite joy's flame that inspires them all.

596: Nurture family and community, find peace in simple moments, and let joy be the mortar that binds your bond.

597: The angels encourage clear and honest communication. Express your needs and desires authentically, listen actively to others, and strive for understanding in your relationships.

598: Know your worth, a star in the celestial tapestry. Receive abundance with open palms, share your blessings like sunlight, and let generosity be your cosmic crown.

599: Uplift and inspire with your spiritual gifts, heal with compassion, and illuminate the path for others.

600: Success doesn't come overnight. Be prepared to put in the hard work, face challenges with determination, and never give up on your dreams. Your angels are supporting your every step.

601: Trust your inner fire, take the leap, and manifest your dreams with unwavering strength. The universe applauds your bold new beginnings.

602: While embracing change and new beginnings, remember to stay grounded. Maintain a sense of stability and practicality to navigate challenges effectively

603: Share your unique talents with authenticity and inspire others with the vibrant dance of your creativity. Remember, the world needs your unique spark.

604: While pursuing your ambitions, don't neglect your spiritual well-being. Explore different practices, connect with your higher purpose, and cultivate inner peace and harmony.

605: The universe reminds you of your inherent strength and resilience. It encourages you to persevere through challenges, stay focused on your goals, and never give up on your dreams.

606: Strengthen bonds with gentle care, find joy in simple moments, and let connection be the fertile soil for your shared happiness.

607: Your gut feeling is your guide. Pay attention to your inner whispers and intuitive nudges, they will lead you towards the right decisions and actions.

608: Make time for rest, self-care, and activities that bring you joy. Be adaptable and flexible in your approach as things may unfold differently than you expect.

609: This message emphasizes the importance of nurturing your spiritual connection. Explore different practices, meditate, and connect with your intuition to deepen your understanding of your purpose and path.

610: Remember to be practical and organized in your approach. Manage your time effectively, prioritize tasks, and avoid distractions to ensure progress towards your goals.

611: Follow passions, express your authentic self, expand your influence. Your creative flame lights the world.

612: Partner with others who share your vision and values. Collaboration can enhance your success and provide support on your journey.

613: Trust your inner whisper, let fear fade. Embrace new beginnings, faith your compass, mind open to alignment.

614: Angels dance beside you, their whispers encouragement. Believe in yourself, a star in the cosmic sky, their support unwavering.

615: Your thoughts and beliefs have a powerful impact on your reality. Focus on positive thoughts and intentions to attract positive outcomes.

616: While experiencing change, remember the importance of maintaining balance in your life. Prioritize self-care, nurture your relationships, and take responsibility for your actions.

617: Dive deep within, connect with your celestial self. Explore wisdom, seek guidance, expand your spiritual understanding.

618: Recognize your worth, a universe of abundance at your heart. Receive with gratitude, share generously, manifest prosperity.

619: This cosmic message carries positive vibrations of abundance and manifestation. Focus your thoughts and actions on your desires, and trust in the Universe to support you in achieving them.

620: Close chapters with grace, lessons learned your guiding light. Release, prepare for fresh perspectives, open your heart to new beginnings.

621: Sometimes, things may not unfold exactly as you envision. Trust in the divine timing and know that even detours can lead you to your ultimate destination. Learn from experiences and keep moving forward.

622: Your life is undergoing a significant transformation, leading to a more fulfilling and aligned version of yourself. Embrace the changes with open arms and trust that they are for your highest good.

623: Unleash your inner spark! Joy and optimism, your brushstrokes of inspiration. Share your unique talents, ignite creative breakthroughs.

624: Change is inevitable and often leads to greater fulfillment. Trust the timing of the Universe and embrace the changes that come your way as opportunities for growth and expansion.

625: Embrace the cosmic winds of change. Release the past, dance with new opportunities. Personal growth blossoms in transformation's embrace.

626: Strengthen family bonds, find joy in simple moments. Home is where love and connection thrive.

627: As you navigate change and manifest your desires, remember to express gratitude for the blessings in your life and share your abundance with others.

628: Recognize your cosmic worth. Abundance flows, receive with open palms, share generously. Manifest prosperity, let blessings bloom.

629: While striving for your goals, remember to maintain balance and harmony in your life. Prioritize self-care, spend time with loved ones, and engage in activities that bring you joy and peace.

630: Sometimes, things may not unfold as quickly as you'd like. Trust in the divine timing and know that your efforts will bear fruit in due course. Patience and perseverance are key.

631: The angels whisper their encouragement! Follow passions, express your true self, influence blooms through your pursuits.

632: While embracing change, ensure you have a strong foundation in place. This could involve financial stability, supportive relationships, or a clear sense of purpose.

633: Listen to your inner whisper. Conquer fears, embrace new beginnings with faith, aligned with your guiding star.

634: Angels dance beside you, their wings carry encouragement. Believe in yourself, a cosmic spark, forever supported.

635: While positive changes are coming, don't just wait for them to happen. Your angels encourage you to take initiative, work hard towards your goals, and create your own destiny.

636: Take time to appreciate the support you receive from others and the blessings in your life. Gratitude attracts more positivity into your life.

637: This divine message signifies a powerful period of transformation in your life. Embrace these changes with an open heart and trust that they are leading you towards greater alignment and fulfillment.

638: Recognize your cosmic worth, abundance flows to you. Receive with gratitude, share generously, prosperity blossoms.

639: Pay attention to your gut feelings and inner wisdom. They will guide you towards the right decisions and actions to take on your journey.

640: While striving for success, remember to maintain balance in your life. Make time for rest, relaxation, and loved ones. Avoid neglecting your physical and mental well-being in pursuit of your goals.

641: Be grateful for the blessings in your life, both big and small. Acknowledge your achievements, no matter how small, and celebrate your journey towards your goals.

642: Don't wait for things to happen to you. Take inspired action towards your goals, guided by your intuition and aligned with your true purpose.

643: Trust the whispers of your creative spirit. Unleash your unique expression, share your vibrant perspective, and paint the world with the colors of your soul. Angels applaud your artistic journey, reminding you that your gifts are a celestial blessing.

644: Take a deep breath, release the grip of the past. Transformation dances on the horizon, urging you to embrace change with open arms. Angels guide your steps through personal growth, whispering promises of a brighter future.

645: Nurture your haven of love, a beacon of warmth and belonging. Strengthen family bonds, find joy in simple moments, and let connection be your guiding light. Angels smile upon your efforts, ensuring your home thrives with laughter and peace.

646: Connect with your higher self, explore divine guidance, and expand your spiritual understanding. Angels light the path inward, revealing the celestial map within.

647: Open your heart to the river of abundance, receive with gratitude, and share your blessings with generosity. Angels remind you that prosperity flows when you give and receive with an open hand.

648: Use your spiritual gifts to heal, inspire, and uplift others. Let compassion be your guiding star, and remember, your service illuminates the path for all. Angels sing your praises, celebrating your acts of kindness.

649: Release what no longer serves, prepare for fresh perspectives, and open your heart to new beginnings. Angels dance beside you, celebrating the closure that paves the way for endless possibilities.

650: Trust the whispers of your intuition, a compass leading you towards alignment. Angels guide your every step, whispering encouragement and ensuring your success.

651: You have the power to create your own reality through your thoughts, actions, and unwavering belief in yourself. Trust your inner strength, take inspired action, and watch your dreams manifest into reality.

652: Collaboration unlocks hidden possibilities. Join forces with kindred spirits, share your strengths, and watch synergy orchestrate success. Angels celebrate the power of teamwork, weaving threads of unity into your shared tapestry of achievements.

653: Express joy with unbridled passion, a radiant beacon in the world. Ignite your inner flame, share your unique laughter, and inspire others with your contagious optimism. Angels sing along to your joyful dance, reminding you that lightheartedness is a celestial gift.

654: Manifestation waits on the horizon, fueled by focused intention and relentless effort. Visualize your goals, take decisive action, and watch your dreams solidify into reality. Angels guide your hands, ensuring your focused energy bears fruit.

655: Embrace the whispers of change, a metamorphosis waiting to unfold. Release outdated patterns, welcome new perspectives, and let transformation sculpt your journey. Angels dance in the chrysalis of your being, celebrating the beauty of renewal.

656: Nurture inner peace, a celestial garden cultivated with self-care and mindfulness. Prioritize your well-being, listen to your needs, and find joy in the quiet moments. Angels tend to your spirit, ensuring your inner Eden flourishes.

657: Seek wisdom beyond the veil, where intuition illuminates the path ahead. Connect with your higher self, delve into spiritual mysteries, and expand your cosmic understanding. Angels guide your exploration, revealing secrets whispered by the stars.

658: Recognize your abundance, a cosmic treasure flowing towards you. Open your heart to receive gratitude, share your blessings generously, and witness the endless cycle of giving and receiving.

659: Heal with compassion, inspire with hope, and uplift the fallen with unwavering faith. Your touch transforms lives, a beacon of love in the darkness. Angels stand beside you, amplifying your service to the world.

660: Be grateful for the blessings in your life, both big and small. Acknowledge your progress, celebrate your achievements, and learn from your setbacks.

661: Pursue your ambitions with unwavering tenacity. Trust your convictions, take bold steps, and witness your dreams become reality.

662: Even amidst change, strive for inner peace and harmony. Practice mindfulness, meditation, or other calming techniques to navigate the transformation with grace and balance.

663: Unleash your creative spirit. Express your unique perspective with authenticity, share your joy like contagious laughter, and inspire others with your artistic audacity.

664: Stay laser-focused on your goals, visualize success with meticulous detail, and watch your dreams solidify into reality. Angels weave celestial threads of support, ensuring your focused energy bears abundant fruit.

665: Embrace the winds of change, a metamorphosis whispering promises of renewal. Release outdated patterns, welcome new opportunities, and let transformation sculpt your journey.

666: Prioritize your well-being, quiet the inner critic, and discover joy in the stillness. Angels whisper encouragement, reminding you that your inner sanctuary fuels your outward strength.

667: You have the power to manifest your desires and create the reality you envision. Focus your thoughts and actions on your goals, and trust in your ability to make things happen.

668: The universe encourages you to embrace change, step outside your comfort zone, and explore new possibilities.

669: Be grateful for the blessings in your life, both big and small. Share your abundance with others and contribute to a more compassionate and supportive world.

670: Release attachments with grace, forgive transgressions with open arms, and open your heart to new beginnings. Angels dance in the farewell, celebrating the endings that pave the way for endless possibilities.

671: Take decisive action, fueled by inner confidence, and watch your dreams manifest under the celestial light. Angels guide your every step, whispering encouragement and ensuring your success.

672: Surround yourself with positive and encouraging people who support your growth and uplift you. Collaboration can smooth the path of transformation.

673: Express yourself and spread the joy of creativity. Angels applaud your artistic expression, reminding you that your gifts are a celestial treasure.

674: Manifestation waits on the horizon, fueled by focused intention and relentless effort. Visualize your goals, take decisive action, and watch your dreams solidify into reality. Angels guide your hands, ensuring your focused energy bears fruit.

675: The universe emphasizes the power of positive thinking and shifting your mindset. Focus on optimistic thoughts, affirmations, and visualization to attract positive experiences and manifest your desires.

676: Nurture inner peace with self-care and mindfulness. Prioritize your well-being, listen to your needs, and find joy in the quiet moments. Angels tend to your spirit, ensuring your inner Eden flourishes.

677: Pay close attention to your intuition and inner wisdom. They will guide you towards the right decisions and actions during this transformative period.

678: The angels remind you of your potential to create abundance in all aspects of your life and encourage you to take action towards your goals.

679: The angels want you to release any worries or anxieties holding you back. With a clear mind and open heart, take inspired action towards your goals and dreams.

680: Closure whispers like a gentle breeze, lessons learned a guiding light. Release attachments, forgive transgressions, and open your heart to new chapters. Angels dance in the farewell, celebrating the endings that pave the way for endless beginnings.

681: Intuition's compass guides, trust its quiet nudge. Align with your soul's purpose, action awaits.

682: Synergy sings in shared strengths, unite with kindred spirits. Your collaboration dances, achievements unfold.

683: Unleash your vibrant spark, let creativity paint the world. Joy's laughter echoes, inspiring all who see.

684: Dreams solidify with focused will, visualize, then strive. The cosmos aligns, manifesting your desires.

685: This message encourages you to explore your spiritual beliefs, meditate, and connect with your intuition. Deepening your spiritual connection can bring clarity, peace, and guidance on your life path.

686: Nurture your inner haven, peace blooms in quiet moments. Self-care waters your soul, joy blossoms within.

687: While embracing change, remember to maintain balance and harmony in your life. Make time for self-care, rest, and relaxation to navigate this dynamic period with grace.

688: Abundance flows, a cosmic river. Receive with open arms, share blessings with generosity.

689: This number signifies a time to connect with your higher purpose and align your actions with your spiritual calling. Trust your intuition and inner guidance to lead you on the right path.

690: Release, forgive, and welcome new beginnings. Lessons learned light your path, endless possibilities await.

691: Your angels are urging you to step out of your comfort zone and take action towards your goals. Don't wait for the perfect moment, start now with small steps and build momentum.

692: Sometimes, the timing of change may not be as you expect. Trust that the Universe has a perfect plan for you and surrender to the flow of life with faith and optimism.

693: Let your creative spirit soar, paint the world with your unique brushstrokes. Joy's laughter echoes, igniting others with your artistic audacity. The cosmos applauds your vibrant expression.

694: Before taking action, ensure you have a solid foundation in place. This could involve financial stability, supportive relationships, a healthy lifestyle, and a clear sense of direction.

695: Embrace the winds of change, let transformation sculpt your journey. Release the past, welcome new horizons. The cosmos whispers promises of renewal, dancing in the chrysalis of your being.

696: Cultivate inner peace, a celestial garden nurtured by self-care and mindfulness. Listen to your soul's whispers, find joy in the stillness. The cosmos grants serenity to those who seek it.

697: The angels encourage you to be clear and authentic in your communication with others. Express your needs, desires, and boundaries with confidence.

698: Major changes are coming your way, but they are meant to propel you forward. Trust that these changes are for your highest good and embrace them with an open heart.

699: Heal with compassion, uplift with hope, be a beacon in the darkness. Your service ignites a constellation of kindness, transforming lives with each touch.

700: Closure paints the horizon with lessons learned, a gentle sunset before new beginnings. Release attachments, forgive transgressions, open your heart to fresh chapters. The cosmos celebrates endings that pave the way for endless possibilities.

701: Trust your inner compass, a star chart within your soul. Navigate with intuition, aligning with your deepest desires. The universe reveals its secrets to those who trust their inner guide.

702: Welcome changes in your life with an open heart. These changes, though they may seem challenging at times, are leading you towards greater personal growth and spiritual fulfillment.

703: Unleash your vibrant spark, let creativity dance across the world. Express your unique laughter, igniting joy in all who witness. The cosmos applauds your artistic soul.

704: Focused will sculpts reality, visualize your dreams with unwavering belief. The universe bends to your intention, manifesting desires like celestial constellations.

705: Don't just wait for things to happen, take inspired action towards your goals and dreams. Trust your intuition and inner nudges to guide your steps.

706: Nurture your inner haven, a sanctuary cultivated by self-care and mindfulness. Listen to your soul's whispers, find peace in the quiet moments. The cosmos grants serenity to those who seek solace within.

707: Know that you are not alone on this journey. Your angels are supporting and guiding you every step of the way. Trust in their divine presence and guidance.

708: You are encouraged to connect with your soul's calling and use your gifts to make a positive impact on the world. Consider volunteering, pursuing a creative passion, or starting a project that aligns with your values.

709: While pursuing your goals, remember to maintain harmony and balance in your life. Prioritize self-care, connect with loved ones, and nourish your physical and emotional well-being.

710: Closure paints the horizon with lessons learned, a gentle sunset before new beginnings. Release attachments, forgive transgressions, open your heart to fresh chapters.

The cosmos celebrates endings that pave the way for endless possibilities.

711: You have the power to create your own reality. Focus your thoughts and actions on your desires, and trust in the Universe to support you.

712: Celebrate differences, weave a tapestry of unity, where all voices find their song. The cosmos hums with the music of acceptance.

713: Unleash your creative spirit, paint the world with your vibrant brushstrokes. Joy's laughter splashes, igniting others with your artistic audacity. The cosmos applauds your unbridled expression.

714: Don't let your ambitions consume you. Maintain a balance between pursuing your goals and nurturing your relationships with loved ones and yourself.

715: Release the past, welcome the whispers of new beginnings. The cosmos dances in the chrysalis of your being, celebrating renewal's embrace.

716: Cultivate inner peace, a celestial garden nurtured by self-love and quiet moments. Listen to your soul's whispers, find joy in the stillness. The cosmos grants serenity to those who seek refuge within.

717: Dive deep into the well of wisdom, where intuition illuminates hidden pathways. Connect with your higher self, expand your cosmic understanding. The stars whisper secrets to those who listen with open hearts.

718: You have the power to attract abundance into your life. Focus your thoughts and actions on your desires, cultivate gratitude for what you have, and trust in the Universe to provide for your needs.

719: This is a nudge to build a solid foundation in your life, whether it's financial security, supportive relationships, or a strong sense of purpose. This provides stability for your growth and success.

720: Release attachments, forgive transgressions, open your heart to fresh chapters. The cosmos celebrates endings that pave the way for endless possibilities.

721: Before taking action, ensure you have a solid foundation in place. This could involve setting clear goals, creating a plan, and developing the necessary skills and resources.

722: It is time to deepen your connection with your inner wisdom and intuition. Pay attention to your dreams, synchronicities, and gut feelings, as they will guide you towards the right decisions and actions.

723: Unleash your creative spirit, let your soul's brush paint the world. Laughter ricochets, igniting joy like wildfire. The cosmos applauds your audacious artistry.

724: Focused will sculpts reality, dreams etched with unwavering belief. The universe bends to your intention, manifesting desires like glittering constellations.

725: Shed old skin, welcome new horizons. The cosmos whispers promises of renewal, guiding you through the time of change.

726: Nurture your inner sanctuary, a celestial haven bathed in self-love and quietude. Listen to your soul's lullaby, find peace in the hushed moments. The cosmos grants serenity to those who seek solace within.

727: Connect with your higher self, expand your cosmic understanding. The stars whisper secrets to those who listen with open hearts and minds.

728: Pay attention to your inner wisdom, dreams, and synchronicities. They will guide you towards the right path and help you make decisions aligned with your higher purpose.

729: With your focus aligned and inspired action taken, your ability to manifest your desires increases. Believe in your power and trust the Universe to support your journey.

730: Closure paints the horizon with lessons learned, a gentle farewell before new beginnings. Release attachments, forgive transgressions, open your heart to fresh chapters. The cosmos celebrates endings that pave the way for endless possibilities.

731: Your creative fire burns bright, intuition your guiding torch. Dare to dream, take the leap, your influence paints the world in vibrant hues.

732: Soulmate whispers fill the air, love's symphony awaits. Build bridges of trust, nurture compassion, together your haven thrives.

733: Fear's shadows fade in wisdom's light, intuition whispers courage. Embrace new beginnings, faith your wings, soar beyond limitations.

734: Angels dance beside you, whispers of support in every breeze. Believe in your divinity, manifest your dreams, the universe applauds your journey.

735: This message suggests a period of heightened spiritual growth and connection. You may experience increased intuition, synchronicities, or a deeper understanding of your life purpose.

736: Nurture your roots, community your garden. Inner peace blossoms, connections flourish, love's harvest overflows.

737: Find harmony between your spiritual aspirations and your earthly responsibilities. Create a life that nourishes both your soul and your body.

738: Use your abundance and talents to help others. Be a source of light and inspiration for those around you, and contribute to the greater good of humanity.

739: Major transformations are on the horizon. Embrace these changes with courage and trust that they will lead you to a brighter future.

740: Closure paints a gentle sunset, lessons learned like guiding stars. Release with grace, embrace fresh horizons, new beginnings dance on the morning breeze.

741: While pursuing your goals, remember to maintain balance in your life. Make time for rest, relaxation, and loved ones. Don't let ambition consume you at the expense of your well-being.

742: The angels are saying it is time to pay attention to your dreams, synchronicities, and gut feelings, as they will guide you towards the right decisions and actions.

743: Unleash your vibrant spirit, let your soul's brush paint the world anew. Laughter spills like sunshine, igniting joy in every corner. The cosmos applauds your audacious artistry.

744: Use your achievements and talents to contribute to the greater good. Serve others, support your community, and make a positive impact on the world.

745: While embracing change, ensure you have a stable foundation in place. This could involve financial security, supportive relationships, or a clear sense of purpose.

746: Nurture your inner sanctuary, a celestial haven woven with self-love and quiet moments. Listen to your soul's lullaby, find peace in the hushed symphony of your being. The cosmos grants serenity to those who seek solace within.

747: Pay close attention to your gut feelings and dreams. 735 encourages you to trust your intuition and make decisions based on your inner wisdom.

748: While pursuing your goals and higher purpose, don't neglect your physical and mental well-being. Make time for rest, relaxation, and activities that bring you joy.

749: The universe empowers you to manifest your desires through your creativity and self-expression. Focus on positive thoughts and actions to attract abundance and fulfillment.

750: Release ties with grace, forgive gently, open your heart to fresh chapters. The cosmos celebrates endings that pave the way for infinite possibilities.

751: Challenges are not roadblocks, but stepping stones to growth. Learn from your mistakes, adapt your approach, and keep moving forward with unwavering determination.

752: Trust your partners, share your strengths, together you harmonize, goals dance towards fulfillment.

753: Joy's laughter spills like wildfire, igniting passions long suppressed. Unleash your unique spark, express your vibrant soul, the world awaits your radiant dance.

754: The universe encourages you to cultivate compassion, build supportive relationships, and take care of those around you.

755: Angels whisper of change. Step outside your comfort zone, learn new things, and evolve as a person. Embrace challenges as opportunities for growth and self-discovery.

756: Nurture your inner garden, cultivate peace amidst life's whirlwinds. Self-compassion waters your spirit, quiet moments bloom with serenity, let your sanctuary blossom within.

757: Connect with your higher self, expand your cosmic understanding through meditation and silent prayer, ancient secrets await your listening heart.

758: Recognize the endless river of abundance, flowing towards your open palms. Receive with gratitude, share with generosity, the universe thrives on your open heart and giving spirit.

759: The universe reminds you to find harmony between your spiritual aspirations and your earthly responsibilities. Create a life that nourishes both your soul and your body.

760: Release attachments with grace, forgive like blooming flowers, open your heart to fresh fields. The cosmos celebrates endings that pave the way for endless meadows of possibility.

761: The angels tell you to pay attention to your gut feelings and intuitive nudges. They will guide you towards the right decisions and actions to take.

762: Explore meditation, prayer, or other spiritual practices to deepen your intuition and understanding of your inner wisdom.

763: Release limiting beliefs, past hurts, or negative energies that are holding you back. Embrace forgiveness and move forward with a clean slate..

764: Set ambitious goals, take inspired action, and trust in your ability to manifest your desires.

765: This message points towards open communication and teamwork. Be receptive to collaborating with others on projects and sharing your ideas.

766: Nurture your inner sanctuary, a celestial haven bathed in moonbeams and whispered prayers. Listen to your soul's lullaby, find peace in the hushed symphony of your being.

767: Remember the importance of prioritizing your physical and mental health. Take time for self-care practices and activities that bring you joy..

768: A thrilling journey is ahead! Embrace new opportunities, explore different paths, and don't be afraid to step outside your comfort zone.

769: The angels speak of positive change, remember that these changes may unfold at their own pace. Trust that the universe has a plan for you and be patient with the timing of its unfolding.

770: The cosmos whispers of closure. Release the old and open your heart to new beginnings.

771: Angel wings whisper courage, intuition your celestial compass. Align with your divine spark, leap with faith, victory dances in celestial light.

772: Harmony resonates in angelic choirs, understanding bridges every gap. Celebrate the diversity, weave a tapestry of love, where differences sing in heavenly chorus.

773: Unleash your radiant spirit, let your soul paint the world with divine hues. Laughter spills like an angel's song, igniting joy in every corner, the cosmos applauds your artistic grace.

774: Nurture your dreams and aspirations with care and attention. Develop a clear plan, gather resources, and take consistent action to bring your goals to fruition.

775: Be patient and trust that the Universe has a perfect plan for you. Even amidst delays or setbacks, stay positive and focused on your goals.

776: Nurture your inner sanctuary, a haven woven with divine whispers and quiet moments. Listen to your soul's lullaby, find peace in the celestial hush, let your spirit bask in angelic serenity.

777: This is a message that your angels are surrounding you with love, guidance, and support. Trust that everything happening in your life is leading you towards your highest good.

778: The angels are reminding you that change is inevitable, and the ability to adapt will be key to navigating this period successfully. Be flexible, open-minded, and learn from your experiences.

779: Heal with a touch of angel's compassion, uplift with a whisper of hope, be a beacon in the darkness, your service paints a constellation of kindness.

780: Release attachments with grace, forgive with angel's wings, open your heart to fresh chapters, blessed by the cosmos.

781: Starlit whispers fill the air, celestial guides nudge you towards your destiny. Trust their twinkling guidance, leap with faith, your path shines like a comet across the velvet night.

782: Trust your gut feelings and inner wisdom as they guide you towards the right path.

783: Expressing gratitude for the blessings in your life. Show appreciation for what you have and share your abundance with others.

784: The universe bends to your unwavering gaze, manifesting desires like galaxies swirling in the celestial night.

785: Positive thoughts and affirmations attract positive experiences, while negative ones can create obstacles. Shift your focus to optimism and gratitude to see your life blossom.

786: Listen to your inner voice, find peace in the cosmic silence, let your spirit bask in the celestial embrace.

787: You will be experiencing significant changes in your life, leading to a more empowered and aligned version of yourself. Embrace these changes with an open heart and trust that they are for your highest good.

788: Deepen your connection with your higher purpose and spiritual truth. Explore different spiritual practices, meditate, and seek guidance from your intuition.

789: This is a strong message that your angels are surrounding you with love, support, and encouragement. They are urging you to move forward with your goals and embrace the journey ahead.

790: Closure paints the horizon with lessons learned, a gentle farewell before new dawns. Release attachments with grace, forgive like blooming nebulae, open your heart to fresh galaxies, blessed by the celestial beings.

791: Angel wings whisper in your ear, intuition your celestial compass. Fearlessly navigate uncertain paths, angel's light guides your every step. Victory dances in your wake, dear one, trust your unwavering spirit.

792: Welcome changes in your life with an open heart. These changes, though they may seem challenging at times, are leading you towards greater personal growth and spiritual fulfillment.

793: Unleash your radiant spirit, let your soul ignite the world with joy. Laughter spills like sunshine, angel's smile beams upon your artistry. Express your vibrant essence, your unique spark sets hearts ablaze.

794: The universe bends to your whispered prayers, angel's hand guides your desires to fruition. Manifest your dreams with celestial confidence,the stars align with your will.

795: Explore meditation, prayer, or other spiritual practices to deepen your intuition and understanding of your inner wisdom.

796: Nurture your inner sanctuary, a haven woven with celestial whispers and quiet moments. Angel's wings brush away anxieties, find peace in the hushed symphony of your being. Within your sanctuary, serenity awaits.

797: Pay attention to your dreams, synchronicities, and inner nudges as they will guide you towards the right decisions and actions. This is a time for growth, wisdom, and understanding.

798: Your gifts and talents are meant to be shared with the world. Use them to serve others, make a positive impact, and contribute to a better world.

799: Embrace changes with an open heart and trust that they are leading you towards a higher purpose and greater personal growth.

800: Release attachments with grace, angel's forgiveness blooms like wildflowers. Open your heart to fresh chapters, the cosmos celebrates endings that pave the way for infinite possibilities.

801: Intuition screams rebellion, dare to be different. Victory awaits your unique spark, rewrite the rules, embrace the maverick.

802: Harmony thrives in diversity, celebrate every voice. Build bridges of understanding, together you shine brighter.

803: Rise from the ashes, laugh in the face of doubt. Unleash your inner fire, joy is your weapon, spread your wings and soar.

804: While pursuing your ambitions, don't neglect your spiritual well-being. Explore different practices, connect with your higher purpose, and cultivate inner peace and harmony.

805: Transformation is your dance, shed limitations, embrace new horizons. The cosmos whispers possibilities, trust the unknown, become who you were meant to be.

806: Inward peace is your haven, let go of burdens, find solace in silence. Angel's grace surrounds you, nurture your sacred sanctuary.

807: Focus your thoughts and actions on your goals and desires with unwavering belief in your ability to make them happen. The Universe is supporting your endeavors, so stay positive and take inspired action.

808: Abundance flows freely, receive with gratitude, share with an open heart. Your generosity blesses the world, remember, giving fuels abundance.

809: Heal with compassion, uplift with hope, be a beacon in the darkness. Your kindness paints constellations of change, touch lives with your gentle glow.

810: Lessons learned paint the horizon, release attachments with grace. Forgive like blooming flowers, open your heart to new beginnings. The cosmos celebrates endings that lead to endless possibilities.

811: Your thoughts and intentions are aligning with the Universe, paving the way for material and spiritual prosperity. Stay positive, focus on your goals, and trust that you have the power to create the life you desire.

812: The angels whisper that a soulmate connection is destined. Nurture new relationships and feel the love blossom.

813: Heed the wisdom whispered from within, a celestial chorus guiding your steps. Conquer fears with the sword of action, a knight's courage paving the way for new dawns. Remain ever aligned with the divine design, a compass etched upon your soul.

814: Angels urge you to tap into your self-confidence and embrace your personal power. Believe in your abilities, make bold decisions, and take ownership of your life.

815: Believe in your ability to manifest your desires. Set clear intentions, visualize your goals, and take inspired action towards achieving them.

816: Build a sanctuary of peace, a haven where community thrives. Nurture the garden of connection, finding solace in the gentle act of service, each seed of kindness strengthening the bonds that bind.

817: While embracing change and pursuing your goals, remember to cultivate inner peace and balance.

818: Believe in your ability to manifest your dreams and goals. Focus your thoughts and actions on what you desire, and trust in the Universe to support you.

819: Let your spiritual gifts be a beacon of lightwork, uplifting others like a celestial sunrise.

820: Closure, a gentle wave washing over the shores of your past, lessons learned like seashells gathered on the beach. Release the burden with grace, for fresh doors stand ajar, promising new chapters woven with celestial thread.

821: Let optimism be your compass, a sunlit path leading to inspired action. Become a beacon of hope, a lighthouse piercing the shadows with the radiant flame of your spirit.

822: This is a reminder of the presence and support of your angels. They are encouraging you on your journey and offering guidance when needed. Trust that you are not alone and reach out for their support when necessary.

823: Let your true self show. Speak your truth and new opportunities will open to you.

824: Build abundance, not just in coin, but in joy and purpose. With faith as your compass and action your steed, conquer your goals and paint your world with the colors of success.

825: Embrace the metamorphosis, a butterfly shedding its cocoon. Let go of the past, a withered leaf falling away, and step into the dawn of personal growth.

826: Nurture your sanctuary, a haven where family bonds thrive. Find peace in the embrace of love, a celestial tapestry woven with threads of warmth and understanding.

827: The angels remind you to prioritize self-care, mindfulness, and activities that bring you joy. Abundance flows best when you maintain a harmonious state of being.

828: Even amidst the excitement of adventure and change, remember to cultivate inner peace and harmony. Practice self-care, mindfulness, and activities that bring you joy.

829: Trust in your connection to the divine and allow your intuition to lead the way. Look to your dreams and trust your instincts.

830: Closure, a gentle sigh as the final chapter closes. Embrace fresh perspectives, pages yet to be written, and step into the dawn of new beginnings.

831: Take decisive action, dear one, guided by the compass of your intuition. Each step, inspired by inner whispers, leads you onward to your divine destiny.

832: Within partnerships, seek balance, a celestial dance where differences dissolve in the gentle music of communication. Let truth be your bridge, a rainbow arching across divides, healing hearts and fostering understanding.

833: Let your authentic voice be a call for positive change. Inspire with the truth that burns within you, a sun igniting the spirit of others with your vision.

834: Faith in your dreams is the fuel that propels you forward. Persevere with trust, for angelic hands uphold you even in the darkest storms. Remember, you are never alone.

835: The Universe supports your efforts when you align your thoughts and actions with your true purpose.

836: Build a safe haven for your friends and loved ones. Be there for others and they will return the favor.

837: The universe encourages you to deepen your connection to your higher self, intuition, and inner wisdom. Pay attention to your dreams, synchronicities, and gut feelings as they guide you on your spiritual journey.

838: Express gratitude for the blessings in your life and the support you receive from your angels.

839: Let your spiritual gifts be lanterns in the darkness, casting the light of healing and inspiration upon the world. As you use your lightworking skills, you become a beacon of hope, guiding others towards their own inner radiance.

840: Closure beckons, a gentle hand closing the final chapter of the past. Learn from the lessons etched upon its pages, and prepare for new chapters yet to be written.

841: Angels guide you towards new beginnings. Embrace the potential that lies within you, and watch as your life blossoms with radiant possibilities.

842: A gentle nudge from angels awakens your goals. They walk beside you, offering support and guidance as you strive to achieve your dreams.

843: Angels whisper encouragement, urging you to embrace change. Just as a caterpillar transforms into a butterfly, you too are called to release the beauty within you.

844: Angels walk beside you, celebrating your journey. Feel their loving presence surrounding you, reminding you that you're never alone.

845: Express your creativity, let your voice ignite, and watch your influence grow. Illuminate the world with your unique spark and inspire others.

846: Build a sanctuary of peace, serve with an open heart, and watch connections deepen. Nurture peace and foster harmonious connections with those around you.

847: Focus your thoughts and actions on your goals with unwavering belief, and trust that the Universe is supporting you in making them happen.

848: Embrace your worth and boundless potential. Receive abundance with gratitude, and share your gifts freely. Recognize your worth and let your gifts enrich the world.

849: This message from the universe carries the energy of manifestation and abundance. Focus your thoughts and actions on your desires and believe in your ability to make them a reality.

850: Close the past with grace, learn its lessons, and embrace the exciting doors of new beginnings. Honor the lessons of the past, but allow yourself to turn the page and embrace new possibilities.

851: Ignite your creative fire, let your unique voice be heard, and expand your influence in the world.

852: Your soulmate connection awaits. Build a loving partnership founded on trust and nurture it with care.

853: Trust the wisdom within you. Conquer your fears with action and embrace the exciting new paths that lie ahead.

854: You are surrounded by angelic support. Believe in yourself and trust the guidance you receive.

855: Express your joy in your relationships. Collaborate creatively and watch your artistic partnerships flourish.

856: Build a loving home for yourself and your loved ones. Never take these relationships for granted. They are truly special..

857: Deepen your spiritual understanding. Explore the wisdom of the universe and seek knowledge to guide your path.

858: Recognize your worth and potential. Receive abundance with gratitude and share your gifts freely with the world.

859: The angels are encouraging you to help others. Your positive vibrations will be echoed by the universe.

860: Learn from the lessons of the past and prepare for exciting new chapters. Release the past with grace and move forward with an open heart.

861: Embrace challenges head-on, find strength within yourself, and overcome obstacles to emerge stronger. A new chapter in your career awaits, ready for your unique voice to shine.

862: Amidst change, maintain balance and harmony in your life. Take care of your physical and emotional well-being, prioritize self-care, and find activities that bring you joy. A balanced life allows you to approach transformation with grace and a positive mindset.

863: Trust your inner wisdom, your guiding compass. Take action to conquer your fears and embrace new beginnings. Remember, your life is aligned with a divine purpose, so stay focused and pursue your dreams.

864: Angels whisper encouragement in your ear. Believe in yourself and your abilities, trusting the guidance you receive from both within and above.

865: Let joy be your driving force in relationships. Collaborate creatively with others, sharing inspiration and watching artistic partnerships flourish.

866: Your positive thoughts and actions are attracting prosperity and wealth. It encourages you to remain focused on your goals, trust the universe's timing, and take inspired action towards achieving your desires.

867: Deepen your connection to the divine. Explore the wisdom of the universe and seek knowledge to expand your consciousness and understanding.

868: Recognize your intrinsic worth and the vast potential that lies within you. Receive abundance with gratitude and share your gifts generously, for prosperity flows freely when generosity leads the way.

869: Use your spiritual gifts to bring light and healing to the world. Be a beacon of hope, inspiring others with your compassion and uplifting them with your radiant spirit.

870: Closure brings clarity and wisdom. Learn from the experiences of the past, then release them with grace. Fresh doors stand open, inviting you to embrace new beginnings and exciting possibilities.

871: Ignite your creative fire, let your unique voice roar, and expand your influence in the world. New career beginnings await, ripe for your passionate exploration.

872: A deep connection to someone new is on the horizon. Build a supportive partnership, a haven where love thrives and understanding flourishes. Remember, trust is the cornerstone of this sacred bond.

873: Trust your inner wisdom, it whispers truth in the quiet corners of your soul. Conquer fears with decisive action, embracing new beginnings as stepping stones to your divine purpose.

874: Change is inevitable and often leads to greater fulfillment. Trust the timing of the Universe and embrace the changes that come your way as opportunities for growth and expansion.

875: While seeking change and growth, don't neglect the importance of a solid foundation. This could involve building financial security, establishing healthy relationships, or developing essential skills.

876: While pursuing material abundance, be mindful of your spiritual and emotional well-being. The angels remind you to cultivate inner peace, nurture your relationships, and give back to others..

877: Embrace the changes coming your way with both courage and wisdom. Be open to new opportunities, learn from your experiences, and adapt with flexibility.

878: Recognize your worth, a dazzling diamond sparkling with potential. Receive abundance with open arms, a chalice overflowing with blessings. Share your gifts freely, for in generosity, prosperity multiplies.

879: Uplift, inspire, and heal with the gentle touch of your compassion. Be a beacon of hope, leading the way towards a brighter world.

880: Closure and lessons learned whisper on the wind. Release the past with grace, for it prepares you for exciting new chapters. Fresh doors swing open, inviting you to embrace new beginnings and limitless possibilities.

881: Unleash your inner rockstar, let your voice shatter expectations, and watch your influence explode like a supernova. Career horizons stretch endless, ready for your audacious paintbrush.

882: Your soulmate, the missing piece to your cosmic puzzle, awaits just around the bend. Build a partnership on the bedrock of trust, a love song where understanding hums like a lullaby.

883: Trust your gut, that wise oracle whispering truth from your core. Conquer fears with a warrior's spirit, embracing new beginnings as stepping stones to your soul's grand design.

884: Angelic whispers brush your dreams, reminding you of your limitless potential. Believe in the symphony playing within you, a celestial map guiding your every move.

885: Let joy be the confetti you sprinkle on every connection. Collaborate with reckless abandon, watching artistic partnerships bloom like gardens bathed in moonlight.

886: Build a haven where kindness is the currency, a community woven from threads of compassion. Serve with open arms, knowing that in giving, your own peace blossoms like a thousand wildflowers.

887: While striving for abundance, remember the importance of spiritual balance. This reminds you that true fulfillment comes not just from material success but also from connecting with your higher purpose and serving others.

888: This message from the angels signifies unlocking your full potential and achieving personal mastery. It reminds you of your capabilities and encourages you to strive for success in all aspects of your life.

889: Your angels cheer you on! Be an example of hope and inspiration to others.

890: Closure arrives like a gentle sigh, the final chapter whispered on the wind. Release the past with the grace of a falling leaf, for fresh doors stand ajar, promising adventures bathed in the golden light of new beginnings.

891: Let your creative force explode, your voice resonate powerfully, and watch your influence ripple through the world. New career heights beckon, waiting for your ambitious climb.

892: Your destined connection is close, a harmonious echo just waiting to be sung. Cultivate a relationship grounded in unwavering trust, where love blossoms under the gentle light of understanding.

893: Heed the wise whispers within, the oracle guiding you from your soul's depths. Confront your fears head-on, and embrace new beginnings as stepping stones to your divinely-guided path.

894: Believe in your own strength and capability, for your potential is limitless. Trust the intuitive whispers that lead you toward your destined future.

895: Angels remind you of the importance of kindness and compassion. Extend these qualities to yourself and others, fostering positive connections and creating a more harmonious world.

896: Offer your service with an open heart, for acts of kindness sow the seeds of peace and strengthen the threads of connection.

897: Your angels are with you on this journey. They assure you of their love and support. Trust that you are guided and protected, even amidst challenges.

898: Embrace abundance with gratitude, a chalice overflowing with blessings. Share your gifts freely, knowing that generosity multiplies prosperity for all.

899: This number signifies a period of significant transformation in your life, leading to greater abundance and prosperity. Embrace the changes, even if they're challenging at first, as they're leading you towards a more fulfilling and successful future.

900: Release the past with grace, for it prepares the soil for vibrant new chapters to blossom. Fresh doors stand open, inviting you to step into a world of limitless possibilities, bathed in the golden light of new beginnings.

901: Optimism is your compass. Take inspired action, be a beacon of hope, and watch your influence grow.

902: Harmony thrives in balanced partnerships. Communicate openly, compromise with respect, and watch love flourish.

903: Express your truth authentically. Your words can heal, inspire, and share valuable wisdom.

904: Before taking action, ensure you have a solid foundation in place. This could involve financial stability, supportive relationships, a healthy lifestyle, and a clear sense of direction.

905: Embrace change, release limitations. Personal growth awaits as you step into new beginnings.

906: Nurture your home, strengthen family bonds. Find peace and joy in the sanctuary of love.

907: Deepen your spiritual connection. Explore divine guidance, seek wisdom, and expand your understanding.

908: The angels want you to recognize your inherent worth and vast potential. Receive abundance with gratitude, and share your gifts generously.

909: Use your spiritual gifts for service. Heal with compassion, uplift others, and be a guiding light.

910: Closure brings clarity and fresh perspectives. Learn from the past, release it with grace, and embrace exciting new doors.

911: Intuition guides your steps. Take decisive action, fueled by the whispers of your soul, and watch your dreams manifest.

912: Balance flourishes within partnerships. Let communication be your bridge, building understanding and strengthening the bonds of love.

913: Speak your truth. It is a call for positive change. Inspire with authenticity, and watch your vision ignite the hearts of others.

914: Faith is your anchor, your guiding light. Navigate towards your goals with unwavering trust, knowing angels walk beside you.

915: The universe encourages you to welcome changes in your life with an open heart. These changes, though they may seem challenging at times, are leading you towards greater personal growth and spiritual fulfillment.

916: The universe encourages you to be open to new opportunities related to career, finances, or personal growth.

Trust your intuition and take action when presented with a promising path.

917: The angels sing of a period of significant transformation in your life. This could involve major changes in your career, relationships, or even your own inner self. Embrace these changes with an open heart and trust that they are leading you towards greater alignment and fulfillment.

918: Recognize the treasure within, a diamond sparkling with boundless potential. Accept abundance with gratitude, and let your generosity flow freely, enriching the world around you.

919: Focus your thoughts and actions on your desires. Believe in your ability to manifest your goals and take inspired action towards them.

920: Closure whispers a gentle farewell, carrying the wisdom of lessons learned. Release the past with peace, for it prepares the fertile ground for vibrant new beginnings to unfold.

921: Embrace challenges as stepping stones. Develop inner strength, overcome obstacles, and emerge stronger and wiser. A new career chapter awaits, ready for your confident exploration.

922: Build a partnership, personal or professional, where trust and understanding resonate like a harmonious melody. Embrace mutual respect and support.

923: Conquer fears with decisive action, embrace new beginnings as doorways to your divinely-guided purpose. Remember, your path is illuminated by your unique potential.

924: Use your achievements and talents to contribute to the greater good. Serve others, support your community, and make a positive impact on the world.

925: It is time to deepen your connection with your inner wisdom and intuition. Pay attention to your dreams, synchronicities, and gut feelings, as they will guide you towards the right decisions and actions.

926: Remember that true abundance goes beyond material possessions and also includes inner peace, love, and meaningful relationships.

927: Deepen your spiritual connection, explore the vast cosmos within. Seek knowledge that expands your understanding, like starlight illuminating your path. Remember, the whispers of wisdom are all around you for those who listen with open hearts.

928: This signifies a period of positive change and transformation in your life. This could involve career advancement, financial gain, or achieving personal goals.

929: The Universe is supporting you, so don't be afraid to dream big and put in the effort.

930: Your thoughts and intentions are aligning with the Universe, paving the way for material and spiritual prosperity. Stay positive, focus on your goals, and trust that you have the power to create the life you desire.

931: Conquer challenges with focus and resilience. Emerge stronger and wiser, ready to tackle new career frontiers.

932: Soulmate whispers draw near. Build a haven of trust and understanding, where love flourishes.

933: Pay attention to your gut feelings and inner guidance when making decisions related to finances or career.

934: Don't just dream, actively nourish your goals and desires with love, dedication, and positive energy. Invest time and effort in making your dreams a reality.

935: Infuse your relationships with joy, collaborate creatively, and watch your partnerships blossom.

936: The universe reminds you to maintain balance and a sense of responsibility even amid positive changes. It encourages you to manage your resources wisely and prioritize your well-being.

937: Delve deeper into your spiritual understanding, seek knowledge, and illuminate your path like a guiding star.

938: Embrace your worth and boundless potential. Receive abundance with gratitude, and share your gifts freely.

939: Let your spiritual gifts be instruments of light. Uplift, inspire, and heal with the gentle touch of compassion.

940: Close the past with grace, learn its lessons, and embrace the exciting doors of new beginnings.

941: Conquer career challenges, climb the ladder of success with focus and resilience. Aim high, and your achievements will soar.

942: New relationships are starting. Build trust, understanding, and watch love blossom in your haven of harmony.

943: Trust your inner wisdom, it guides you towards your divine purpose. Embrace new beginnings, conquer fears with decisive action.

944: Angels whisper encouragement, believe in yourself and your path. Trust the intuitive whispers that guide your future.

945: You have the power to manifest your desires. Focus your thoughts and actions on what you truly want and believe in your ability to make it happen.

946: Build a sanctuary of peace, serve with an open heart, and watch connections deepen within your community.

947: Pay attention to your dreams, synchronicities, and gut feelings, as they will guide you through this period of transformation. Trust in your connection to the divine and allow your intuition to lead the way.

948: Embrace your worth and boundless potential. Receive abundance with gratitude, and share your gifts freely.

949: The universe urges you to deepen your connection to your higher purpose and use your talents to serve others. This can bring immense personal growth and fulfillment.

950: Close the past with grace, learn its lessons, and embrace the exciting doors of new beginnings.

951: Unleash your creativity, let your voice ignite, and watch your influence grow. New career horizons beckon, ready for your ascent.

952: Pay attention to your gut feelings and inner guidance when making decisions related to finances or career.

953: Conquer fears, embrace new beginnings. Your inner wisdom guides you, decisive action paves your path.

954: While ambition is important, don't neglect your emotional and spiritual well-being. Seek fulfillment in meaningful relationships, personal growth, and service to others.

955: While embracing change and pursuing your goals, remember the importance of a solid foundation. This could involve financial stability, healthy relationships, or a strong sense of purpose.

956: This number signifies a period of positive changes and new beginnings in your life. It could be related to your career, finances, relationships, or personal growth.

957: Focus your thoughts and actions on your desires and believe in your ability to make them a reality.

958: Embrace your worth and boundless potential. Receive abundance with gratitude, share your gifts freely.

959: Practice self-care, mindfulness, and activities that bring you joy. Cultivating resilience will help you bounce back from any challenges you face.

960: Release the past with grace, learn its lessons. Embrace new beginnings, step into exciting possibilities with an open heart.

961: Ignite your inner fire, let your voice resonate with passion, and watch your influence ripple through the world. New career heights beckon, ready for your ambitious climb.

962: Harmony thrives in balanced partnerships. Communicate openly, respect each other's needs, and watch love blossom in a haven of mutual understanding.

963: Speak your truth authentically, your words can be powerful tools for healing, inspiration, and sharing valuable wisdom.

964: Faith is your anchor, your guiding light. Navigate towards your goals with unwavering trust, knowing angels walk beside you.

965: Embrace change, release limitations. Personal growth awaits as you step into new beginnings with a courageous heart.

966: Nurture your home, strengthen family bonds. Find peace and joy in the sanctuary of love and connection.

967: Deepen your spiritual connection, explore the vast wisdom hidden within. Seek guidance, expand your understanding, and let it illuminate your path.

968: Find balance between your spiritual aspirations and your material goals. Don't neglect your spiritual well-being in the pursuit of success.

969: This message encourages you to set ambitious goals, take inspired action, and trust in your ability to create the life you desire.

970: Closure whispers a gentle farewell, carrying the lessons learned. Release the past with peace, for it prepares the fertile ground for vibrant new beginnings to unfold.

971: Unleash your creative fire, let your voice resonate powerfully, and watch your influence grow. New career heights beckon, ready for your ascent.

972: Soulmate whispers draw near. Build trust, understanding, and watch love blossom in your haven of harmony.

973: Trust your inner wisdom, it guides you towards your divine purpose. Embrace new beginnings, conquer fears with decisive action.

974: Angels whisper encouragement, believe in yourself and your path. Trust the intuitive whispers that guide your future.

975: Appreciate the blessings in your life and share your abundance with others. This opens up the flow of positive energy and attracts even more good things into your life.

976: Build a sanctuary of peace, serve with an open heart, and watch connections deepen within your relationships.

977: The Universe is supporting you in achieving your goals, so don't be afraid to set ambitious dreams and take inspired action.

978: Embrace your worth and boundless potential. Receive abundance with gratitude, and share your gifts freely.

979: Your celestial guides encourage you to connect with your higher purpose, use your talents for the greater good, and trust your inner wisdom.

980: Release the past with grace, learn its lessons. Embrace new beginnings, step into exciting possibilities with an open heart.

981: Your unique talents shimmer like hidden gems, waiting to be unveiled. Angels whisper encouragement as you express your soul's gifts, watching your spirit blossom beneath the sun of self-discovery.

982: A symphony of passion plays within you, a melody yearning to be shared. Angels walk beside you as you step onto the stage of life, enriching the world with your vibrant performance.

983: Open your heart, a vessel overflowing with the potential to heal. Angels guide your gentle hands, leading you towards paths where wounds find solace and burdens lighten.

984: New doors creak open, bathed in the golden light of possibility. Angels whisper encouragement as you embrace your soul's gifts, stepping into adventures yet to be written.

985: Decisive action paints your canvas, fueled by the whispers of angels urging you to manifest your deepest desires. Watch as your dreams take vibrant form, brushed with the strokes of courage and faith.

986: A tapestry of understanding unfurls as you share your gifts with the world. Angels illuminate your path, revealing intricate threads of connection that bind you to others in meaningful ways.

987: Let the whispers of angels guide you towards positive change, and watch as your authentic bloom paints the world anew.

988: Your soul-guided goals shimmer on the horizon, beckoning you forward. Angels walk beside you, offering unwavering support as you climb towards your destined summits.

989: New beginnings sprout like wildflowers in the wake of your shared light. Angels guide your path, ensuring each step you take nourishes the fertile ground for personal growth.

990: Love's sweet melody surrounds you as you embrace your soul's purpose. Angels celebrate your journey, showering you with blessings and joy each step of the way.

991: A gentle nudge from angels awakens your potential. Embrace new opportunities with courage, for they hold the keys to fulfilling your soul's purpose.

992: Whispers of love and support surround you as angels guide your path. Trust in their presence, for they illuminate the way towards harmonious relationships and heartfelt connections.

993: Conquer fear with the strength of a thousand angels at your back. Step boldly into unknown territories, knowing that divine guidance empowers you to overcome any challenge.

994: The universe celebrates your journey, showering blessings upon each step you take. Embrace it's encouragement as you navigate life's twists and turns, trusting in the unfolding of your divine plan.

995: Let your creativity dance in the moonlight, guided by the celestial muse. Angels rejoice in your artistic expression, inspiring you to paint your dreams onto the canvas of reality.

996: Build a sanctuary of peace within your heart, a refuge where angels find solace. Share your compassion with others, and watch as healing blossoms in the warmth of your kindness.

997: Angels speak of financial stability, supportive relationships, and a clear sense of purpose. A solid foundation will provide you with the strength and stability you need to navigate the changes coming your way.

998: Abundance flows towards you like a golden river, guided by the generosity of angels. Receive with gratitude, and let your blessings overflow, nourishing the world around you.

999: Angels herald a time of endings and new beginnings. Embrace the closing of cycles with grace, for they pave the way for extraordinary transformations and limitless possibilities.

I hope all of your dreams become reality. Hearing your experience makes it worth it

Scan the QR code to leave a review for
Angels Numbers and Divine Numberology

Preview the New Book by
Sarah Ripley

The Symphony of Manifestation: Why 3, 6, and 9 Hold the Key to the Universe.

Nikola Tesla, the visionary inventor, once uttered a cryptic yet intriguing statement: "If you only knew the magnificence of the 3, 6, and 9, then you would have a key to the universe." These enigmatic numbers, woven into the fabric of his 3-6-9 manifestation practice, have sparked curiosity and debate for decades. But what truly lies behind their significance?

Imagine the number 3 as a bridge, gracefully arching between your individual consciousness and the boundless energy of the cosmos. In many cultures, three symbolizes completion, creation, and the divine trinity. For Tesla, it represented the direct link to the "Source," the universal force that governs all existence. By focusing on the number 3, you open yourself to this cosmic reservoir of power, paving the way for manifestation.

Think of the number 6 as a hidden vault, unlocking the depths of your own potential. In numerology, 6 is associated with balance, harmony, and responsibility. For Tesla, it signified the deep well of strength hidden within each individual. By repeating the number 6, you tap into this internal reservoir of resilience, courage, and determination, empowering you to overcome obstacles and push through limitations on your path to manifestation.

"If you only knew the magnificence of the 3, 6, and 9, then you would have a key to the universe."

- Nikola Tesla

Picture the number 9 as a phoenix rising from its ashes, representing transformation and renewal. In numerology, 9 symbolizes completion, compassion, and letting go. For Tesla, it signified the act of releasing the baggage of the past, including self-doubt, negativity, and limiting beliefs. By focusing on the number 9, you clear the emotional clutter that impedes your progress, allowing you to step into a fresh cycle of possibility and pave the way for your desires to manifest.

The Power of the 369 Method lies not just in the individual numbers, but in their harmonious orchestration. Repeating affirmations throughout the day creates a rhythmic resonance, tuning your mind to the frequency of the universe. It's like playing a cosmic melody, attracting your desires into existence through the power of focused intention and unwavering belief.

Remember, the true key to unlocking the universe lies not just in understanding the numbers, but in embodying their essence. Embrace the connection to the Source, harness your inner strength, and release any negativity that holds you back. With dedication and practice, the 369 Method can become a powerful tool for shaping your reality and manifesting your deepest desires.

About the Author

Sarah Ripley is a certified Life Coach, mentor, and author of books and journals on relationships, self-help, spirituality, and natural healing. She is also a trained Chakra healer, Naturopath, and Master Herbalist.

Sarah has a passion for helping others to live their best lives. She believes that we all have the power to heal ourselves and create the life we want. Her work is focused on helping people to connect with their inner wisdom and intuition, and to develop the tools and skills they need to live their lives in alignment with their values and purpose.

Sarah has traveled throughout Asia, South America and Europe studying different cultures and spiritual beliefs. She is also a nature lover who has done extensive trekking in the Himalayas, Rockies and Andes Mountains. She is a passionate advocate for natural living and enjoys cooking with a completely natural diet. She spends her free time relaxing with her family and cats.

Sarah has been married for 28 years and has 2 adult children. She currently lives in Southeast Asia with her husband and 4 adopted street cats, where she continues to write, teach, and mentor others. She is also working on a new book about her experiences with natural healing and spirituality.

Made in United States
Orlando, FL
16 February 2025